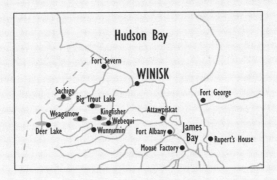

The village sits in its pearl-grey dome,
A child has turned it upside down,
All the snow is falling!

The Village Sits
Mildred J. Young
Winisk, May 2,74

An untouched forest as seen from the air.

WINISK

On The Shore of Hudson Bay

Mildred Young Hubbert

Natural Heritage Books

Winisk

On The Shore of Hudson Bay
Published By Natural Heritage / Natural History Inc.
P.O. Box 95, Station O,
Toronto, Ontario, M4A 2M8

Design by Steve Eby

Printed and bound in Canada by Hignell Printing Limited, Winnipeg,
Manitoba

Canadian Cataloguing in Publication Data
Hubbert, Mildred Young

Winisk : on the shore of Hudson Bay

Includes index

ISBN 1-896219-35-7

1. Hubbert, Mildred Young.   2. Teachers - Ontario - Winisk -
Biography
3. Winisk (Ont.) - Biography.   I. Title.

FC3099.W573H8 1997   917.13'1   C97-931836-X

F1059.5.W573H8 1997p

THE CANADA COUNCIL | LE CONSEIL DES ARTS
FOR THE ARTS | DU CANADA
SINCE 1957 | DEPUIS 1957

Natural Heritage / Natural History Inc. acknowledges the support received
for its publishing program from the Canada Council Block Grant Program.
We also acknowledge with gratitude the assistance of the Association for
the Export of Canadian Books, Ottawa.

A Note to the Reader

The author was not well when attempting to deal with certain aspects of her final manuscript. Any errors or omissions brought to the attention of the publisher will be corrected in subsequent editions.

Every attempt has been made to be faithful to the author's style and manuscript preferences, including her episodic rather than chronological approach to chapters.

Severn Lights

A curtain of undulating haze
Ignites the Severn sky: –
A shifting shawl of weaving rays
To guide true lovers by.
Flickering stars and shimmering lights
That from the ice caps shine,
Reach out to meet the northern nights,
And lead your hand to mine.

The window on the polar world
Will darken all to soon,
Till then its curtains loose, unfurled,
Are pinned back by the moon;

So shine upon my love and me,
And gently light our way,
Until the northern night shall see
A shining northern Day!

Mildred J. Young
Winisk
October 1971

Dedicated to
Muriel Simpson
who helped to make the project possible.

Square Ones

People come in too many shapes
      and too many sizes,
Milling about in the city–
There are lean ones, and mean ones,
And tall ones, and small ones,
And fair ones, and spare ones, –
Of a multitude of hues
From their heads down to their shoes.

When the wild wind blows and the
      sun shines cold,
The North has a comforting, gentle uniformity,
Everybody looks like a square, blue box –
With rubber boots.

The whole world would be more
      comforting a place
If everyone were built
Like a square blue box –
With rubber boots.

Mildred J. Young,
Winisk
January 8/74

TABLE OF CONTENTS

A NOTE FROM THE AUTHOR

This book deals with a community that no longer exists, having been swept away in 1986 by a horrendous flood that claimed the lives of two native residents.

Though the village of Winisk that was my home for three eventful years in the early 1970's is no more, the former residents have adjusted to a transition which now finds them living roughly thirty-two kilometres up river, at a northern settlement known as Peawanuck (Cree for flint). Adept at surviving in a wilderness environment that would unnerve and defeat many others, the Winisk Cree are a remarkably adaptable people. They are true survivors in the fullest sense and inherently well-equipped to make their way into the 21st century.

On the following pages readers will find a very personal account of my own cherished association with the Winisk community and with the people who for a time were my dear neighbours. The story of such a unique place and people is in my view well worth recording, which is why I chose to turn my hand to what may well be my final book. *Winisk: On The Shore of Hudson Bay* is a personal and hopefully important document of a special place that was with us for centuries, until fate decreed otherwise, such a short while ago.

Mildred Young Hubbert
Markdale, Ontario
March 1997

PREFACE

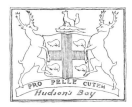

Throughout the long history of Canadian exploration, the area in Ontario between the railway line and Hudson Bay was largely ignored until well into the 20th century. Annual ships' packets of the Hudson's Bay Company made brief visits to the settlements on the coast, first travelling directly from Britain, and later from Moosonee where they loaded their goods and supplies that had arrived by rail from southern Ontario. But the tundra south and west of the James and Hudson bays was so inhospitable and empty that few adventurers attempted to brave the extreme climate, the swampy terrain and the myriad of biting and sucking insects.

The Native people of Winisk, part of the Cree nation that ranges from James Bay to Alberta, speak an Algonkian dialect similar to that spoken from Newfoundland to the Rocky Mountains. Before European contact, those along the coast were a semi-nomadic, gathering people, probably never very numerous in population. The family was the only economic and quasi-political unit, without leaders as such, except for the occasional expert hunter or shaman.

Families moved with the seasons, like the animals on which they depended. Much time in the spring was spent along the coast in search of water fowl. Those living on the periphery of the treeless area followed the caribou out into the tundra. Inland bands came together at good fishing, hunting and berry-picking spots. Autumns would be spent along the coast in search of geese. Inland locations were chosen for winter dwellings as the climate there was less severe, wood would be abundant and the chances of finding beaver, caribou and good ice fishing would be best. The uncertainty of such a gathering economy meant that famines were not uncommon and often severe.

The first Europeans to visit the coast were probably Captain Thomas James and Captain Luke Foxe and their crews, whose ships met near the mouth of the Winisk River in August of 1631. Captain Foxe travelled east around Cape Henrietta Maria and then sailed home to England. Captain James, whose name designated the southern Bay and who also gave the Cape its name, sailed southward to spend a winter of incredible hardship on Charlton Island. The next summer he returned to the Cape where he went ashore and erected a cross with the coat of arms of the king and of the city of Bristol from which he had first set sail.

In spite of the hardships of overland travel, between 1727 and 1815, various Hudson's Bay men made remarkable overland journeys connecting the posts on Hudson Bay to those down the coast of James Bay. Many of them wrote precise and interesting descriptions of their travels.

In most remote settlements the Hudson's Bay Company would first establish a trading post. This would encourage the Native people to congregate at its doors at least for the summer months to sell their furs and to trade for European goods. When the number of families was sufficiently large, missionaries would establish a church and then the government would take steps to provide services, especially in the fields of health and education.

At Winisk there was a reversal. In 1882 the Hudson's Bay Company opened a summer trading post near the mouth of the Winisk River, but it was not until 1901 that a permanent post was established there. The advent of the airplane changed this impasse to some degree when the various northern institutions—the Hudson's Bay Company, the church and government establishments made air access imperative.

With the creation of a summer post at Winisk, the people gathered to socialize and to trade their furs for European goods, the guns, traps and other implements which would totally revolutionize their economy. Clothing and containers of all kinds were changed. The design and materials of shelters were altered. Food, especially flour, lard and tea, not only altered their diet, but could be used to tide them over during lean periods.

After a winter trapping in the bush, families in late May would return to the post to trade their catch and buy new provisions for the following winter. The remainder of the summer would be spent socializing with other families, friends and relatives, as well as repairing possessions for the next trapping season, cutting wood and guiding the occasional visitor. Much time during early June and September would be spent goose hunting. By the end of the hunting season the Native people would leave the post for their winter trapping grounds.

In 1892 a Roman Catholic church was built at Fort Albany and, one year later, at Attawapiskat. In 1895 one-week visits were made by the Oblate priests from Albany to Winisk until a church and rectory was built there in 1900. In 1924 a permanent mission was established at Winisk. This was followed in 1948 by a sawmill and later a recreation hall and a school for summer classes.

Government involvement with the Cree people of Winisk and around the bay began with the signing of sections of Treaty Number 9 in 1905. In 1912, when the boundaries of Ontario were established, the James and Hudson Bay Lowlands came under the jurisdiction of the provincial government. Federal government involvement became more pronounced in the 1930's with the initiation visits to the settlements by members of the Royal Canadian Mounted Police (RCMP). They were followed later by Indian agents and others concerned with the social and medical welfare of the Cree people.

Another major change came to Winisk in late 1954 when work on the Mid-Canada Line, a series of radar stations built along the 55th parallel, was started. Much of the materials and equipment were brought in during 1955 - 56, mainly by sea via Hudson Strait from the south and from the railhead at Moosonee. During both the construction and operation of the radar line many Native people were employed as wage labourers at the base, positions which many preferred over the rigours and uncertainty of the trapline.

The Royal Canadian Air Force 408 Squadron and Air Transport Command personnel were stationed at the larger sites such as Winisk, swelling the population to seven hundred labourers. When the Winisk site was completed in 1957, the population shrank to one hundred and fifty-nine. By 1965 when the whole system was closed down, because of the improvements to the Pine Tree Line farther south, the Native people were forced to return to their more traditional ways of living. By now they had been altered irreversibly by their new grasp of English and by their close contact with a radically different way of life.

The village of Winisk had been established in a flood plain and every spring was in danger of being swept away by both the water and the icebergs trying to reach Hudson Bay. If the ice at the mouth of the river broke up first, all was well since the effluence from upstream could stream smoothly past the village and out to sea. However if the ice broke first upstream, which was farther south, and the ice remained intact at the river's mouth there was nowhere for the ice and water to go but to spread out over the surrounding lowlands, inundating everything in its path.

The big flood of 1967 swept away most of the Native houses and even the Hudson's Bay store, located a mile or more back into the bush and willows. The basement of the teacher's house (then owned by Lands and Forest) and the mission basement were both full of water right up to the floor boards of the first floor. At that point a serious discussion was held to consider moving the village to a safer location, but no consensus could be reached

But the most disastrous flood occurred in the spring of 1986 when water and icebergs destroyed the village, killing 76 year old John Crowe who did not have time to get into his canoe. It also took the life of Margaret Chookomoolin who tried desperately to save the youngest of her three children by holding him above the icy water as her sister tried to reach them in her canoe. The sister did manage to grab the baby and pull him to safety, but the mother disappeared under the water and was swept away. This flood convinced the villagers never to return to the Winisk site, but to stay with relatives and friends in Attawapiskat until a village could be built on a new site.

Today the community of Peawanuck, with a population approximately two hundred and forty, is located thirty-two kilometres up river from the former village of Winisk. Seventy-two residential units are supported with other community buildings such as residences for nurses and teachers, a clinic, a general store, a local radio station, a diesel powered electricity generating station, a Ministry of Natural Resources Park Office, Ministry of Transportation airport and fueling facilities and a newly built elementary school. All buildings have water and sewage service.[1]

THE ODYSSEY BEGINS

"Isn't this wonderful?" he enthused as we sped through the waves.

It wasn't a bit wonderful. George crouched in the bow of the canoe, his prominent nose cutting the wind while a sheet of icy water swelled over the side and drenched me to the skin. Vainly I tried to wipe the water from my glasses. Already I had come to an early conclusion that there was little to see, beyond the dark Winisk River sliding around the many islands that clustered at the river's mouth. In the far distance a thin line of river bank barely could be seen, topped with match box houses and cones of drying wood. That faint outline constituted the village of one-hundred and fifty Native people that was to be our home for the next three years.

Alex Hunter, the chief, sat impassively at the stern, guiding the canoe over shoals and around obstacles of various kinds, his view of the teacher's new wife quite unfathomable. Eventually we reached the dock on the far bank and sloshed up through the mud to the house. George and Alex followed, laden with boxes of items I thought essential for survival near the coast of Hudson Bay.

"You are coming into a well equipped house," George had assured me. I knew better. The house had been a male enclave for years and a man's view of items required for survival consisted of a passel of guns and a sleeping bag.

What I required for survival were towels and sheets, and place mats, and books, especially cook books since my culinary skills were pretty sketchy. Survival also included a typewriter and a sewing machine and other odds and ends. We did have electricity of a sort, manufactured by a mechanical device called "a generator" which was housed in a shack at the far end of the village. The local priest also had a generator, but just a tiny three kilowatt affair which produced about as much power as a candle. It was used only when our generator collapsed with overwork and died in its tracks, as it did rather often. Then it would take a holiday until some person clad in overalls arrived on one of the bi-monthly planes or on a charter, to dive into its mysterious innards and coax the creature back to life.

1

The Hudson Bay Lowlands from the air.

The road through Winisk village.

The house itself was quite attractive for a northern dwelling, having been built some years before by the Department of Lands and Forests for use of their personnel when they visited the area. Birdseye maple furniture once had made the interior cosy, but by the time I arrived all the fancy stuff had been transported to other venues and the house had to make do with a motley collection of government items. None was originally intended for a remote village in the wilderness, situated five miles upstream from the shores of Hudson Bay in order to avoid the salt water tides.

To have expected that one item might have matched another was of course absurd. The kitchen had a useful propane stove which boasted the only oven in the village. There was a sink into which ran a stream of water that Alex pumped up periodically from the river into holding tanks in the basement. We were in the lower section of the village where the run-off from the upper end flowed past our house with the current and constituted our water supply. Up stream also was an early graveyard which was gradually being eroded by the spring runoff, leaving graves sticking out of the river bank like drawers. One coffin was broken open, revealing a slim body in a black serge suit such as might have been worn around the turn of the century. Both the body and the suit were well preserved because of the years spent in the permafrost. Eventually Father Daneau had the exposed bodies reburied in the newer graveyard, located beyond the far end of the village.

I seemed to be the only person in the village who did not drink the river water in its original state, but boiled vigorously all drinking water or put halazone tablets in it. I did notice, however, that I survived no better than anyone else.

There was a useless propane fridge in the kitchen and a much better electric one in the dining area. I opened the latter with some anticipation, but found that all it contained was some bacon and eggs and a frozen owl, lovingly preserved in all its feathers until Lands and Forest personnel should arrive to claim it. Why would they want it? Apparently there was some great significance to a Snowy Owl being found on the shores of Hudson Bay where one had never been reported before. George, an avid bird watcher, kept telling the village people to leave the birds alone, but whenever they shot or captured some interesting species they brought the creature to him to dispose of as he saw fit.

That winter they brought us a enormous bald eagle which George housed in a crate in the basement. There it lived in apparent contentment, fed by small boys who brought the entrails of their hunting for it to eat. Through most of the winter it sat on its perch intently regarding my inept efforts to do the laundry a few feet from its quarters, its slitted eyes checking each item that went in and out of the wash.

In early spring the men from Lands and Forest did arrive and with surprising enthusiasm transported the bird to their wild life sanctuary somewhere in the south. I actually missed the great creature, but hoped it would be happy in its new quarters.

The house contained a pleasant sitting room with a huge window overlooking the river through which the September sun streamed all afternoon. Before freezeup it framed a constantly changing scene of boats, planes, dogs and people, all of which came and went up and down the busy river and the high path that ran above it. If we looked downstream towards the Bay, we could see the tops of the icebergs that rose with the tide, then sank out of sight again as the tide receded.

The livingroom furniture, such as it was, was arranged in rows around the walls as though in a furniture store awaiting purchase. The curtains, whose original colour might have been green, no doubt had hung in the same spot undisturbed for years. George regarded me with astonishment when I took them down for washing.

"How could curtains get dirty just hanging on the wall?" he wanted to know. I felt I had no satisfactory answer to that question.

After taking inventory, I suggested that it might take us about a month to really clean the house to a satisfactory state.

"A month?" George exclaimed, "I thought a couple of afternoons after school would do it."

It would have helped if we had had a broom of course, but a broom was not a northern requisite—lots of guns and fishing poles but no broom.

Three bedrooms opened off a short hall, all of them crowded with a multitude of beds and mattresses. True to bureaucratic practice nothing matched anything. There were springs with no headboards or supports; there were mattresses with no springs;

there were single beds but no single mattresses or springs. Eventually I took all the springs and arranged them on the floor of one bedroom. Onto them I spread all the mattresses I could find, making one large square bed that virtually covered the entire floor. Of course the mattresses were of different thicknesses which made a very uneven surface, but with the sheets spread over them in layers, and sleeping bags and the few blankets I could find to place over them, they made a very satisfactory bed.

George was delighted with this arrangement, declaring that it was the first time he had ever had a bed that accommodated his six-foot-four frame with any degree of comfort. Of course in the morning the bedding usually ended in a heap on his side of the floor, since he tended to roll himself in whatever covered him as he used to do in his trusty sleeping bag. Very early I learned to brace my chilly feet against his back and, with mighty heaves, return at least some of the bedding back to my side of the bed. When we eventually returned south I insisted on twin beds where I could roll up in my own blankets without a nightly fight for what was mine.

The house also had a bathroom, but because of the need to conserve water, the toilet could only be flushed at infrequent intervals and the bath filled to minimum level. The bathroom also sported a delightful looking shower head, but since no water flowed from it, I decided reluctantly that it was only for show. I later gathered that the sewage from our house flowed untreated into the river, past the houses below us and eventually found its way out to Hudson Bay. This was an arrangement that concerned me, but I didn't know what to do about it.

Besides the holding tanks in the basement, an oil furnace down there warmed the house, but in case it might fail, a space heater sat in the livingroom as a backup. Our fuel was oil, contained in huge drums that sat on the river bank in front of the house ready for instant use and flown in at intervals. One spring when the river flooded at breakup time and inundated the basement, the space heater proved a real blessing.

Next to our house, forming what you might call the business section of the village, stood the red roofed buildings of the Hudson's Bay Company—the warehouse, the store itself and the

A view of Winisk from the frozen river. The three white buildings
on the left were built by the Hudson's Bay Company—staff house,
store and warehouse. The store later burned down. The white house
on the right is the teacher's home.

house for the manager, at that time a young, single man fairly new
to the Company. He was later joined by a Scottish lad who had
been whisked out of Scotland to Montreal and flown immediately
up to Hudson Bay. There he could not conceal his bewilderment
at his new surroundings, while the village people could not conceal their puzzlement at his accent which we felt would have been
improved by the use of sub titles.

At the far end of the village was the Mission, presided over by a
physically small Oblate priest called Father Daneau. He lived in a
tall, white house with bedrooms upstairs to accommodate passing
travellers. Downstairs was an enormous kitchen, dominated by a
wood stove that produced most of the heat for the building and
filled it with the pungent scent of crackling wood and roasting
caribou, or goose, or whatever the village people had brought to
offer to the church.

A few years before our arrival some outraged villager had set the
original church on fire and it had never been rebuilt. Consequently
services were held next door in another large white building, half
of which constituted the church and half the school where George

presided. Father Daneau said Mass every evening and several times on Sunday, all services well attended. The church section of the building was a sparse room with walls of chipboard made from wood chips pressed into an adhesive. The floor at one time had been painted gray, but over the years had been worn by the rub of many moccasins and rubber boots. The church was furnished with plain grey benches with backs, but with more backless benches piled against the walls. The altar at the front was neat and orderly with its draperies, statues and candles, all warm and gleaming in the morning sun. Although a small electric organ was available it was rarely used and, instead, an elderly Native woman with a kerchief on her head would sound the first few notes and lead in the slow, deliberate pace of the singing, all in Cree, of course.

According to Native custom the women and children (and I) sat on one side of the room with the men on the other. George and I always attended because George said we had to support Father Daneau even though we were not Roman Catholics. Accordingly every Sunday we joined the procession that straggled out of the houses and up the muddy trail, many of us in the northern uniform of blue parka and rubber boots. All the older women wore kerchiefs on their heads and clean, printed, cotton dresses hanging below their coats. The younger women wore knitted toques, jackets and slacks. The young children, with a predominance of boys, were swathed in layers and layers of coats, pants, scarves and hats. They would amuse themselves by squirming and twitching and swinging on the backs of benches and generally interfering with one another whenever possible.

Father presided at the service as solemnly as if he were in St. Peter's in Rome. Since the church service was incomprehensible to me, Father gave me a little booklet with English translations so I could follow what was happening to some extent. When it was over, the men filed out first, followed by the women and children, each family dropping off into its home along the trail.

One young couple sadly returned to their home. They had just come back from Hawley Lake, bringing their dead infant who had been buried in the village graveyard the previous week. They were a young couple, scarcely out of their teens, clean, slim and bright. The cause of the infant's death was unknown.

A rutted, gravel trail ran along the top of the river bank with Native houses on each side. A row of hydro poles followed the road from the Mission to our house to provide electricity to these buildings and to the Hudson's Bay Company. Though it ran right past the Native houses it did not generate enough power to serve them, so the people had to rely on either coal oil lamps or more likely, candles set on Carnation milk cans which gave a feeble but gentle light.

We did have telephones that connected the houses of the village, but did not reach beyond our little enclave. In the mission Father Daneau operated a radio phone that snapped and crackled as he sent signals out through the atmosphere when weather conditions were right.

"Do you read me? Do you read me? Over!" the first caller would say, then wait for the reply: "Roger, Roger, I read you loud and clear. Go ahead. Over" Thereafter each speaker took turns in talking, ending each speech with "Over" to indicate it was the other fellow's turn.

In most instances, of course, when the caller said, "This is Winisk—Winisk calling..." whether the call was to Cochrane or Moose or wherever, the only reply would be a lot of rude static which indicated that "the signals are out." The call would have to be made at another time, when the signals were just as likely to still be "out." In case of an emergency, of course, this could be a serious problem.

Father Daneau's first language was French, but he was also completely fluent in English and Cree. He could operate the radio phone in any of those languages as most of the priests did up and down the bay. Father also could read and write the syllabic in which many of the church books were printed. He came regularly to the school to teach the children to read and write the language they already spoke. No television had penetrated the village to this point and radios operating on batteries only brought spasmodic renderings of English programmes. George taught in English and periodically brought in English movies, but outside of these intrusions Cree prevailed almost unaltered from the beginning of time.

This trip was actually not our first attempt to reach Winisk that fall. The day before we had arrived in Timmins at midnight, then boarded Austin's DC 3 to Moosonee at 7:30 the next morning. We had planned on buying considerable groceries in Moosonee, but because of a railway strike, the shelves at the HBC store were pretty bare. Saturday we boarded an ancient Canso from which the seats had been removed and replaced by a narrow wooden bench that ran down one side of the plane. The rest of the space was filled with cargo piled from floor to ceiling, held in place by nets of heavy rope that secured the multitude of boxes, to prevent them from flying around the plane, should there be an emergency landing.

George and I were the only passengers, held in place by narrow seat belts that fastened us to the wall, but seemed more for show than for safety. A young boy in rumpled jeans and bush shirt did his best to act as a sort of steward, disappearing for long periods into the cockpit, then reappearing with a dreadful liquid that he said was coffee. I disputed the assertion, but drank it more for warmth than sustenance.

Seated in this conveyance was like travelling in an ice cold oil drum where both conversation and sleep were out of the question. Since we sat with our backs to the wall, we could not even look out the windows even if there had been anything to see but the miles and miles of bush and muskeg and hour after hour of nothingness. Rain began to fall, not only outside the plane but also inside, adding neither to our comfort nor our state of mind.

Eventually I looked at my watch and shouted to George that I thought the plane had turned around and was heading back to Moose, although there had been no obvious change that we could discern. When our boy again appeared we put the question to him which caused him to nod quite cheerfully in acquiescence. Apparently the plane had started out that morning from Moose, hoping to land at Winisk but, because the signals were out, the pilot had been unable to obtain a weather report. When we, therefore, arrived at the Winisk air base he found that weather conditions made landing impossible. All he could do was turn the plane southward and, after some six hours flying time, we arrived back at Moose from where we had started that morning.

The next day we would try again.

HERE COMES THE BRIDE

———— ◼ ————

"We're getting married this afternoon!" he announced as he burst into my Toronto apartment. "Get me the Yellow Pages and I will find a clergyman."

I looked up in astonishment. I was getting the food ready for a send-off party for a teacher of Native Indian children at the tiny village of Winisk on Hudson Bay. I paid little attention to this bizarre comment since I knew that no one could be married in this abrupt fashion, whether the intended were willing or not. I continued with party preparations, at the same time hearing the conversation on the telephone.

"No, we don't have a licence. No, we don't have a ring," Eventually came the comment, "Yes, 8:00 o'clock will be fine. We'll be there."

"We'll be where?" I wanted to know. George had apparently contacted a clergyman who had some special hot-line to some government official who agreed that if the documents were forwarded the following week to his special attention, he would approve the marriage. The clergyman had explained that these two people wanted to get married (at least one of them did) and the man, or perhaps both of them, were going back north the following day where there was no one on the shores of Hudson Bay to perform the ceremony. In those days 'living in sin' was not an acceptable arrangement, especially for teachers. Perhaps the fact that I was in my mid-forties and George over fifty was a determining factor in the official's acquiesence.

However, by this time I was totally bewildered. I hardly knew this fellow, a six-foot-four teacher, who after four and a half years in the wartime army and a stint at University, taught Indian children and wrote poetry. I acted as a Classroom Consultant with the Deptartment of Indian Affairs from my office in Toronto, making regular visits to the Indian schools throughout the province. I had never visited George, partly because his school was so remote and partly because of his comments some of the teachers had repeated to me.

"Do you know what that fellow said?" one of them told me. "He said to read very carefully the stuff that that lady sends out as teaching suggestions, and then do exactly the opposite and you will be all right."

I was quite affronted and decided I would leave him and his school alone. Then one summer day he swung into my Toronto office, his curly head just brushing the top of the door. Under his arm was a bundle of poetry that he had written during the many years he had spent in the northern bush. I knew his salary was generous, yet his clothes seemed too small for his gaunt frame and there were holes in the soles of his size 14 shoes. He acknowledged that he needed new shoes and could find none in the Salvation store. Always he had outfitted himself at the same time as he bought bundles of clothing for the Native children in his school.

When northern teachers came south I was used to helping them in all sorts of ways, so did not hesitate to accompany him to Eaton's. He was delighted with the size 14 shoes the store actually stocked. In the north the Native women usually made him moccasins out of moosehide. Once one of the women handed him a pair with the wry comment: "Here! Each foot one moose."

I saw little of him the rest of that summer, but in the fall thought that perhaps I might visit his school after all. One bright September day I started off from Moosonee in a small, single engine Cessna with the pilot and a Guidance Counsellor who had business on the way.

George seemed very happy to see us. We would have to stay over night, of course, and George offered us the hospitality of his house since the Mission where visitors usually stayed, was closed. The two men, however, did not think much of having to sleep either on a couch or on the floor in sleeping bags, but opted to move to the Hudson's Bay house where they would be offered a bed. That left me in the house with George.

George was delighted and said that I could have his bed while he would sleep on the couch. This was too compromising a situation for me, so I sent him with his sleeping bag to join the others. There he slept on the floor under the kitchen table accompanied by the ribald comments of the other visitors. A year would pass by before I visited him again, this time dropped off by a passing plane.

Usually on these visits I would stay at the Mission in the village, but since Father Daneau was away on church business, the Mission again was closed. This time I had no alternative but to stay with George. Although he had been happy to have me for an overnight stay the previous year, he seemed to think that any lengthy stay would be regarded by the Native people with a dim view. However, there was nothing else for it even though George kept a discreet distance throughout. The plane did not return for over a week during which I spent my time in the classroom and helping to get the rather meagre meals.

One day, while I was washing up the noon dishes, George looked out the window and cried:

"Oh look! There's Father Daneau! When you finish the dishes we'll go and get married."

I was offended! Nobody got married "when you finish the dishes." And I eventually left Winisk in a huff.

Father Daneau roared with laughter years later when I told him about George's proposal.

"Of course you don't get married when you 'finish the dishes," he said. "If he had said to get married before you do the dishes it would have been all right."

George frequently spent the summers on the farm of his brother, Carman, helping him bring in the hay and do other farm chores. Now and then he would drop in to see me in Toronto for very brief visits. One September day he phoned me from Moosonee on his stopover between Toronto and Winisk.

"When I come down at Christmas we'll get married," he announced, at which suggestion I burst into tears. Instead of being understanding and sympathetic, George asked me if I had seen the famous Russian-Canadian hockey game that had been played that week end.

"What game?" I sobbed, "I don't know anything about a hockey game and I don't want to know anything about it."

"But this was a great game," George explained with enthusiasm, "Didn't you see (whatever his name was) score the winning shot in the last few seconds?"

"I don't know anything about a hockey game," I sobbed brokenly, "and I don't want to hear about it."

This seemed to surprise George, but he went on, "There is quite a group of nurses here just now waiting to go further north. I took one of them to the movies last night."

That cut my sobs off right smartly. George had just proposed marriage to me then announced he was taking out one of the northern nurses.

"What do you mean you took out one of the nurses?" I demanded, "You stay away from those nurses."

My objections seemed to surprise him no end. "Oh" was all he could think of in reply.

After that I heard nothing whatever from George until he entered my life again during the next Christmas break. Suddenly he appeared on my doorstep the night I was going out to a party with friends. The friends were surprised but pleased to have me bring him along and introduced him as 'one of the northern teachers.' Then there he was the following morning, on my doorstep stating that we were getting married that afternoon as soon as he could find someone to perform the ceremony.

"Why didn't you mention getting married the night before?" I asked him some time later

"I didn't think of it the night before," he replied, which seemed to explain everything

Much to my amazement I found myself at the door of this particular clergyman's house and actually at the door of a whole new life. The gentleman showed us down into his recreation room.

"Where are your witnesses?" he asked.

I supposed that they were all at home sitting rather morosely around my living room wondering where the hostess was. When we left home I had asked my neighbour if she would let my guests in when they arrived, since George and I had to "step out for a few minutes."

When they clergyman summoned his wife and his mother-in-law to act as witnesses, the latter demanded that we take our shoes off.

"Your feet are muddy," she pointed out.

There in an unfamiliar basement room, in my stocking feet, I was married to this strange man whom I hardly knew. Life would never be the same again.

Our unsuspecting friends at home, of course, went into

hysterics, both laughing and crying at the same time when we returned to the apartment and someone noticed a ring on my finger. Eventually they served the food, such as it was, "And then you can all go home," George murmured, which they did.

The next day George amused himself by phoning all of his unsuspecting eight brothers and sisters and asking, "Would you like to speak to the wife?" The question was met with shock and disbelief, since none of them expected George to ever get married or even that he had a girl friend.

That afternoon I saw George off on the train that would take him to Moosonee and then the plane north. Months later a young teaching couple told me that on the train George had taken charge of their young baby, walking up and down the corridors with him and pointing out the sights along the way.

"We thought he must be a grandfather with a crowd of young grandchildren," remarked the mother, "We never dreamed he had just been married the day before, and for the first time."

When George reached Moose Factory he called in to see the District Superintendent who was lying on a couch in his home, suffering from a painful back problem. He was a great friend of George's and welcomed him while apologizing for not getting up. George said it didn't matter and he had just come to tell him that he and I had got married.

"That's nice," murmured Mr. C, groaning a little as he moved.

A few minutes later he opened his eyes, looked at George and remarked, "You know, George, I must have drifted off there for a few minutes. I dreamed that you came in and said that you and Millie were married."

"That's what I did say," George replied.

Mr. C. stared for a moment in disbelief then, totally disregarding his sore back, struggled off the couch and danced around the room with the delighted George.

"It's the best news I've heard in years," he declared.

Commitments in Toronto kept me at home, so there I stayed, trying to sort out my life. When I went back to the office people asked the routine question of whether I had had a nice holiday.

"Yes," I replied, "I got married." Stunned disbelief greeted this news. Little work was done for some time as the news flashed across the north where both George and I were well-known. As for me, only the ring on my finger convinced me that something alarming had occurred.

One day I went to the North York Public Library where I announced to the lady at the desk that I had just got married, changed my name and therefore needed a new card. The woman reached for a card, poised her pen and asked, "Yes, and what is your name?"

As I looked at her a panic gripped me when I realized I didn't know what my name was. Nobody had asked me before and I never actually thought about it.

"It's—it's—Mrs...," I stuttered but could go no further. The more she stared at me the more confused I became. Of course I must know what my name was. Everybody knows their names, but obviously I did not know mine. Eventually the lady handed me the blank card.

"I can tell," she concluded, "You're in love. Write out the card when you think of it."

I had never been so embarrassed and decided immediately to fill in the form with whatever my new name was so I could keep it handy for future reference.

Once the smoke cleared, life went on much as it did before—I in Toronto and George at Winisk on Hudson Bay. My Regional Superintendent, however, when he had recovered from the shock suggested that I pay a visit to Winisk—"to investigate staff relations." George was the only one on the staff, but that designation made the trip official and paid for by the Department.

Accordingly I set out from Moosonee one cold February day on the regular DC3 that travelled the coast every other Tuesday. Before I left Moose Factory I called in to the hospital where a group of Indian ladies met me laughing and said, "Now we see you we believe that George is married. He said he was before but we didn't believe him." One lady threw her arms around me and said it gave her renewed hope for herself, "If you can get married, anyone can," a statement which left me a little nonplussed. Then she added, "For a wedding present we'll give you a Band number," which sounded lovely but I never got it.

At the Indian Affairs Branch office the girls gave me a little reception with clapping and cake and coffee. Nobody could remember that I was no longer called Miss Young, nor could I myself.

On the plane I sat with a little Indian girl who had on a wedding ring just like mine. We exchanged experiences re marriage, rings and men. I bought a quart of milk at Moosonee to give to George and kept it in the freezer of the Polar Bear Lodge where I had spent the night. In the plane the next day I put it on what I thought was the floor, but it apparently was the heater. By the time I reached Winisk the milk was scalding hot.

At Attawapiskat a bearded fellow clambered on board the plane to see "Mrs. Hubbert." He said he had gone out with George a year ago when George was transporting a live eagle for Lands and Forest. He said he was "much impressed," and gave me a whiskery kiss. The agent for Austin Airways also came on board, looked me over with a twinkly eye and left again.

At the Winisk landing strip the usual crowd was assembled with their snowmobiles to meet the plane and transport the mail and other goods across the five mile stretch of frozen river to the village. They were not particularly impressed by a new wife; the other goods on the plane were far more important.

George was there all excited, lifting me down before the steps could be rolled up to the plane door. He then introduced me all around as "his wife" then got me inside the hanger to keep warm. A Native man who had arriaved to service the diesel units also descended from the plane and asked where he could stay.

George had me very quickly bundled into a sleigh behind a ski-doo loaded with mail and supplies for the long, cold run across the river to the village. The mail bags and I, the new wife, were all stuffed into the box-like structure. Being attached to the skidoo, we seemed to move at an alarming rate, being bounced and jostled and shaken over the humps and bumps of the frozen river and through the bushes on the banks.

"Stay with us," George invited happily, "The house is full of people. One more won't make any difference."

'Full of people?', I thought. What was the house doing full of people when this supposed to be my 'honeymoon' and the only one I was likely to have.

Finally we arrived. When I entered the house half a dozen or so

men were all sitting around the livingroom looking somewhat disconcerted. They were service men of various kinds coming and
going on diverse northern errands.

"George told us you were coming," they offered, "and he said
we were to clean up the house. We've worked real hard and we
hope it's all right."

I assured them it was just fine as I tried not to see the stacks of
newspapers and oddments of northern paraphernalia piled everywhere. If I opened a drawer I encountered boxes of gun shells and
fish hooks. If I shifted a piece of furniture fishing rods fell on my
head. The Hudson's Bay manager looked in and said that the
house didn't look like the same place since the last time he saw it.
I could only imagine what it was like before the so-called cleanup.

The first night after school I went with George to visit some of
the people. At the first house three children were there alone,
their father being on the trapline and their mother in hospital.
The oldest girl, who was about twelve, stayed home to look after
the house while the two younger ones went to school. Under the
window was a table covered with oil cloth and around it a few
chairs. Across wooden beams near the ceiling mitts and socks were
drying, along with a caribou skin, paper thin and translucent,
ready for tanning. Chunks of wood were drying by the stove and
nearby sat a pail of water that had been carried up from the river.
This house, like all the others, had a porch full of wood, axes, traps
and a motley collection of outdoor items.

The sleeping rooms each had a bed covered with quilts and one
had a dresser. Under the beds were a number of suitcases in which
the people stored their belongings. When George had come in
after Christmas he had brought a doll for one of the little girls in
this home. She held it up for me to see. The older girl had
received a pile of comic books.

In the second house was an elderly couple, the woman with her
eyes squeezed shut with age. George gave her a knitted head scarf
and spoke to both of them in Cree. The old man asked George to
fix a flashlight that he said wouldn't work, so George took it home
to work on it.

In another house the father had just brought home a box full of
suckers he had caught in the river. Nearby a dog was tied, snarling

and barking at visitors. At that moment the elderly woman of the house arrived, dragging two small trees which she had cut down with an axe and was bringing home for the fire.

In the last house were two young women who spoke flawless English and looked somewhat European. A tiny child played about the floor and clung to the legs of one of the women. George had brought each of them a black dress that they had asked for when he went out, and they seemed most appreciative.

On our way to the far end of the village George stopped at the rectory to give Father Daneau a pie he had baked from some kind of mix he had bought somewhere. They discussed a fourteen-year-old boy called Peter who had not been to school for some time. Before we returned home we stopped at Peter's house to determine the reason for his absence. Peter, a stout boy, was sitting on a bed and limped whenever he tried to move. He said that there was a pain in his knee joints and ankles that went up through his groin, although he had not cut his foot or his leg. George hurried home to get a thermometer with which he found that Peter's

Father Daneau, left, the Hudson's Bay Company manager, center and George Hubbert, right. Winisk, 1973.

temperature was 101. He told the boy to stay in bed, then gave the information to the priest who would relay it to the hospital at Moose Factory.

Peter's house was neat and clean, although there were six children ranging in age from Peter down to a baby in a tikinagan, all living in the three rooms. The father tended all of them efficiently while the mother was at Moose Factory in hospital.

There was another boy in the village about the same age as Peter who never went to school. George asked his father the reason.

"Eldon don't believe (in school)," the father explained.

"Well, I guess you've got to believe before it will do you any good," George acknowledged and Eldon stayed at home.

On the weekend George took me on a long walk through the bush and back to a little frozen lake beyond the village. It wasn't too cold as the sun was shining cheerily on the snow and bush that stretched to the horizon in all directions. We followed the skidoo trails that ringed the village, as you would sink to your waist in the snow if you tried to cut through the bush without snowshoes. George tied a couple of targets to a tree and took a few shots at them with his rifle. The tree was so hard with the frost that one shell ricochetted off the trunk and we could hear it zing off to one side, too close to us to be comfortable.

When we were near home we could see that Alex had pulled up to his house with a frozen caribou on his sleigh. The day before one of the girls sold us a hind quarter of caribou, so tender you hardly needed a knife to cut it.

For the two weeks of my so-called honeymoon I cooked for the household of men while George went off to work. Since the food stock was so limited I served them numerous variations of bacon and eggs, to which were added chunks of cheese which I also found in the fridge. I actually had brought several boxes of muffin mix with me, but could find no muffin tins in which to bake them. I had no doubt that someone had taken the tins in which to sort bullets or fish hooks or nails. Determined to carry on, I poured the mix into paper cups which flattened out as they baked and turned into muffin cookies instead of muffin muffins. The men, however, were not critical, but said they were good and ate them all.

The men slept all over the house on couches and in sleeping

bags and on whatever sort of mattresses they could find. It seemed that, although there was no one at our wedding, a good crowd joined us on the honeymoon.

When the plane returned I went back to Toronto and, except for a few days during the Easter break, did not see George again until the following summer.

TO SCOUT THE TERRITORY

---◼---

The year 1973 was not the first time I had visited Winisk. A few years before, while serving as Classroom Consultant with the Department of Indian Affairs, I flew to the little Indian village three-hundred and thirty air miles north west of Moosonee to accomplish two tasks. The first was to determine if the house that Lands and Forest wanted to sell was worth buying, in the hope that a teacher would eventually live in it. Secondly I was to see whether a day school could be opened in the village, so the children would not have to leave home to go to the residential school at Fort Albany for their education.

The Department was very anxious to get out of the residential school business for good reasons. It was much more expensive to house, feed and clothe a child in a residential school as compared to providing day school education while he remained at home. As well, the government was extremely sensitive to the criticism being levied against residential schools, mostly by southerners (both Native and white), some of whom had limited understanding of these institutions. Other information would become available later.

I, therefore, flew up the western James Bay coast in a little single engine Cessna one bitterly cold February day, along with Jack, the Guidance Counsellor, and Michel, the pilot. We followed the shoreline that separated the endless expanse of white, on one side patterned with scrub trees and on the other side, bald to the horizon with white.

Not long out of Moosonee we ran into an area of warmer, misty weather which forced Michel to fly low over the trees to avoid the clouds. Later he explained that this was his first trip on the west coast and he did not realize how close he was to the ground. The Quebec side of the bay, where he had done most of his flying, grew much taller trees. This comment was not very comforting, even though I was trying to sleep curled up on the luggage in the tail of the plane. The two men occupied the two front seats where they could enjoy the meagre warmth of the engine, but no warmth

21

Winisk as seen from the air in winter.

whatever reached the plane's tail. Beyond the haze the temperature dropped to zero degrees Fahrenheit inside the plane. The
temperature outside the plane was anybody's guess.

After a brief stop at Attawapiskat and another two and a half
hours flying time, we reached the air base at dusk. Here Michel
hoped he could keep his plane in the heated hangar over night. At
one time this base had been a busy part of the Canadian Pine Tree
Line established by the United States as one of a row of bases
across the top of Canada. This 'line' offered a warning should the
Russians ever attempt to invade by way of the North Pole. A large
hanger was still maintained along with an extensive air strip, now
used as a stop-over for planes flying chiefly between Churchill and
Canada's eastern Arctic. Although the base itself was long since
closed, the main hangar and some of the buildings still were maintained also as a goose camp to house hunters and as a support for
the bi-monthly planes of Austin Airways that brought mail, supplies and passengers, weather permitting.

In the gathering dusk we landed on the runway and rumbled up to the hangar. The runway was meant for wheels and we were on skis, but a thin covering of snow eased the landing. Unfolding ourselves from our icy compartment, we hurried into the warmth of the hangar. Here we were kindly received in true northern fashion by the caretaker and a group of men doing survey work. The Hudson's Bay Company manager was there also, muffled to the chin in a pair of overalls with what looked like some sort of mattress underneath. Two tiny husky pups snoozed under one of the chairs.

The ensuing discussion concluded that if we left the plane at the base we would have to travel by snowmobile five miles across the frozen river to reach the village. It was apparent that none of us was dressed for such a journey. If the plane had come down in the wilderness in an emergency landing we would have been in a sorry state. Michel, therefore, decided to try to fly over the river and land on a small lake behind the village before complete darkness fell.

The light was almost gone as he buzzed the village to let the people know we were arriving, and set down in a rather bumpy landing on the surface of a small lake fringed by scrub willows. In no time we were surrounded by snowmobiles. One was towing a box sleigh into which Jack and I, along with the gear, were tossed unceremoniously before the whole contingent took off through the bush. Michel sat on the back of one of the other skidoos, hiding his face in the driver's back as protection against the icy wind.

"Your nose is turning white," Jack warned me. I pulled my woollen toque down over my face and just held on as the sleigh heaved over humps in the trail and swerved around sharp corners. I could see nothing but my boots if I chanced to open my eyes.

As we reached the village, the blue haze of a northern night had settled over the settlement, the candle lights of the houses hanging like fireflies in the dusk. Against the still pink sky the smoke from the chimneys rose straight up in the air which was eerily calm in the Arctic cold. If a house were inhabited, the chimney smoked. A cold chimney indicated that the family was away on the trapline, the children probably at school at Albany.

At that time Father Gagnon presided at the mission where he

received us warmly, even though his usual housekeeper was away at Moosonee and he was managing on his own. He assigned each of us a room upstairs, mine a small one with an insulated pipe coming up through the floor for heat. Otherwise heat rose through a grating in the hall floor.

Not unexpectedly the generator was not working. Light was supplied by propane gaslight supplemented by candles placed strategically here and there. Of course, since the electric pump would not work either, Father had to dip water by hand from the reservoir in the basement. The wood stove in the kitchen held a big pot of boiled caribou. He quickly whipped up some powdered potatoes and, with my help, set the table with the caribou meat. A candle was placed in the centre. Father also had some bread from Albany, tinned butter, a can of Carnation milk and a package of Christmas cake. For desert he served canned pears—a totally satisfying dinner and we were cosy and warm.

When we just finished eating two men from the Bell Telephone Company, wrapped like mummies, appeared out of the night. They were there to do maintenance work of some kind, but immediately they set to work to deal with the obstinate generator. In no time at all they had it going, explaining that they thought the gas line had iced up, always a likely scenario in that weather.

Since the men had arrived just as Father was going next door to say Mass, I helped the men get their supper. They had brought their own food—tomatoes, lettuce, steaks, eggs and so on, all items virtually nonexistent in the north.

While they ate, Jack and I washed the dishes, all the while listening to the stories the men were telling of life and sudden death in the wilderness. When Father returned, he joined them. They told about snowmobiles going through the ice; how two men drowned from an overturned canoe when they set out to retrieve a drifting boat; how somebody's body was picked up at Paint Hills on the east coast after he drowned at Moosonee two hundred and sixty miles to the south of there. Father told about the latest flood at breakup the previous year and showed us the high water mark on the basement wall, a few inches below the first floor.

We sat in the kitchen as it was the warmest place in the house. I brought a rocking chair in from the parlour and all was quite cosy, even though the temperature was some fifty-five degrees below zero outside. When the men started playing cribbage, I went to bed.

"What time should we get up in the morning?" I asked.

"Get up when you like," said Father, intent on his cards, "You're at home."

Father himself got up about six a.m. and I could hear him downstairs flinging wood into the kitchen stove and getting things warmed up for the day. While he was out saying morning mass, I got up and set the table. On his return, he cooked the bacon and eggs, while I made toast on top of the stove.

Following breakfast we set out, with René as interpreter, to visit each family that was still in the village. Did the people want to have a day school at Winisk so they would not have to send their children to Albany any more? There were a variety of replies, all indicative of sound reasoning and a far better understanding of the situation than any number of experts in the south.

The village houses were a type of prefab, transported over the ice from the radar base after the original houses had been destroyed in the disastrous flood of the year before. Each consisted of one big room heated by a small wood stove. Beside the stove would be a big oil drum full of melting snow for their water supply. On one stove a pan of bannock was baking and an elderly grandmother went into gales of laughter when I asked if I could take a picture of it. Several beds of one type or another, covered with a motley assortment of blankets were ranged around the walls. Usually there was a table under the window that looked out on the trail, with one or two chairs nearby, and perhaps a cupboard for dishes and pots and pans. Some walls displayed an assortment of rifles. Here and there skins were being cured. In one house was a lynx just thawing out. One had a beaver pelt complete with claws, tail and head although the insides were gone.

Most of the homes contained a mother, a father and several young children. If there was a baby, it was swinging in a hammock strung across the corner of the room or leaning against the wall in a tikinagan. Often an elderly grandmother or grandfather was also present, the former doing beadwork of one kind or anther.

René was intrigued by my interest in the hammock for the babies.

25

"Don't you people have this kind of thing for your babies?" he asked.

Not wanting him to think we neglected our children, I explained the principle of the cradle. He nodded gravely and seemed to think this a sensible sort of arrangement.

Some of the houses had been divided into smaller compartments to create tiny bedrooms to give some privacy. One house had a small room fitted up as a sitting room with living room chairs ranged around a coffee table, probably salvaged from the air base. The owner was a handsome man, probably in his mid-thirties, who said, through the interpreter, that he had never been to school but had picked up a little English by working at the base. He said he knew how important education was and he wanted his children to get as much as possible. He would even like to learn to read and write in English himself. In his pocket he had a Bell Telephone bill but would have to get someone, possibly Father Gagnon, to read it for him. He said his three oldest boys were at Albany, but two more were at home, aged six and seven years, plus a baby of four months. This little fellow regarded us with his big brown eyes, taking in everything that was going on around him. The older boy of this group came in while we were there, wearing a great, white hat of rabbit fur which must have been extremely warm.

Jack asked the man how he felt about a day school on the reserve. Like most of the others he said that he loved his children very much and didn't like to send them away, especially the little ones. He said that he had not sent the two boys aged six and seven because he had lost several children as babies and he hated to let the others go. I asked why the babies died, but he said he didn't know.

"He says his wife goes to Moose Factory to have the babies," René interpreted, "and they seem all right when they come home. But after a little while the babies die and he doesn't know why."

One time this man had been to Ottawa for reasons that were somewhat obscure. I think he had been to Moose Factory and the only plane coming to Winisk was leaving from Ottawa. Somehow he got the train to Ottawa, but had nothing to eat, not even a cup of coffee, for two days because he did not know how to ask for it. This impressed upon him how important it was to learn English and how to read and write. The man's brother lived with his family in the house next door. He had gone as far as grade six at the Albany residential school and his wife as far as grade seven.

Like these two families, most of the Winisk people said they disliked sending their children away to residential school, especially the little ones. Most had lost young children and loved the ones they had dearly. However, they expressed a high opinion of the Albany school and of the education their children were getting there. One father said he would like a school in the village if he could be sure that the teacher would be as good as those at Albany. From my experience with spasmodic attempts at summer schools, this was a shrewd observation. Another said he would prefer to keep his young children at home, but would send the older ones out anyway because their destiny lay in the outside world. The sooner they stepped into it the better.

In two houses grandmothers were looking after small granddaughters while their families were away on the trapline. One elderly lady said she didn't want to send the child away to school because when she was young and having children she lost all of them except one, this child's father. She wanted to keep the little girl as long as possible, but eventually she knew the child would have to go.

All this conversation was conducted through René who had gone to a residential school when he was young. He said that the people at Winisk had really only been in touch with the outside world for the past ten years when the air base and radar site were built. For the first time they had come in contact with families who lived differently and whose children did not die of unknown causes. They wanted to learn how to do the same. Education seemed to be the key, although it was a foreign concept to most of them.

On the way back to the Mission we visited the abandoned classroom that had at one time housed a brief summer school. Christmas decorations were still up on the walls and it looked as though no one had been in the room since the celebrations. Without heat, all the classroom walls, doors and ceilings were thick with frost that glittered in the morning sun. As I took pictures, René suggested that I tell the southern people that this was the way the classroom looked with the stove going full blast. His dark eyes twinkled at the thought.

When we had finished the rounds of the village, we returned to the Mission where Father Gagnon had a huge Canada goose roasting in the oven. He also had a pot of potatoes boiling on top. But as he was swishing around the room, his cassock caught on the handle of the pot, sending it crashing to the floor along with the water and all the potatoes. Father was considerably distressed, suggesting that we get out the powdered potatoes and make a new batch.

"Never mind, Father," I assured him, "the boys are out and they will never know the difference." I got down on the floor, pursuing the errant vegetables under the table and chairs until they were all safely back in the pot and the water mopped up. When the men arrived, they ate heartily.

All through dinner we could hear the radio phone sounding its staccato messages and the frequent ringing of the telephone which Father usually answered in Cree. One fellow had seen me on the trail and wanted to know if I was a nurse. Father commented when he hung up that when there was no nurse around nobody got sick. One man did come in with a badly frost bitten wrist which Father treated rather roughly, I thought, with a salve that looked like vaseline.

The chief joined us for dinner along with René who still acted as interpreter, although Father Gagnon could have served just as well. The main difficulty in setting up a local school was accommodating the children of people who went out for long periods on the trapline, usually from October until after break-up in May. Some came home for Christmas and some did not. They couldn't afford to pay people to keep their children in the settlement while they were away and they couldn't afford two establishments. Besides, they needed their wives' help in dealing with the animals they trapped.

Could they board their children with other families who stayed in Winisk? The chief said that only the old people stayed in the village and they couldn't look after children since they had a difficult enough time looking after themselves. Father Gagnon reminded us that the people loved their children too much to leave them with just anyone.

We asked if the government could subsidize the mothers and children, providing them with wood and food in the settlement while the fathers were away on the trapline. But there was always the danger that once the goods were provided that the men would not leave either, but would stay at home and help use them up. The priest said that the best hunting was a hundred miles and more away and if the wives and children were in the village, the men would move closer and closer until eventually no more trapping would be done at all. All these comments I duly recorded for presentation at our central office in Toronto.

The next morning we were up before daylight to get ready to leave, the weather still desperately frigid. Now that the maintenance men had gone, the generator was not working again. Father had left some candles burning on the kitchen table and the wood stove snapping merrily while he was next door saying Mass. It was still dark outside, but I could just make out the thermometer hanging outside the kitchen window. There was no mercury in it beyond a tiny trace at the bottom. The lowest the thermometer could record was forty below (which is the same in either Celsius or Fahrenheit). Beyond that mark the temperature was anybody's guess. At least the sky was clear and it was shaping up for a fine day.

Michel went off early to heat up the plane by putting a canvas tent over the nose and applying a sort of blow torch to the motor. While this was going on, Jack and I arrived, drawn behind the same skidoo that had brought us in. On the way the driver stopped at the Hudson's Bay store where we were supposed to pick up the weather report. As usual the signals were out so rather than a weather report we got the manager's vague opinion that he thought the weather would hold at least as far as Attawapiskat. If it didn't, there was nothing but two-hundred and thirty miles of ice and snow between.

We arrived at the plane while Michel was still inside his tent with all sorts of gear spread around on the snow. At that point I noticed that my sleeping bag was missing, probably having fallen off somewhere in the village. I thought of the people back there watching us as we sped by.

"They need it more than I do," I thought, "so I won't worry any more about it."

But our skidoo driver insisted on going back for it, and before I could object, jumped back on his skidoo and disappeared down the trail. It was not long before he was back, all smiles, with my sleeping bag. It was obvious that he had never once thought that anyone might take what did not belong to him. I was ashamed of having suspected these people of motives that applied only to my own.

Eventually Michel got the plane's motor started, resulting in a great shaking of the fuselage and wobbling of wings. At that point our Indian friend waved good bye and headed back home, as he now felt that all was well with us and we were on our way. But even though the motor was roaring, the skiis were still frozen into the snow. Jack and Michel had to stand, one at each wing, and rock the plane back and forth to break it loose. Eventually their efforts were effective and the plane finally was moving along the snow. The windows, however, were badly frosted and before the plane could get airborne, it veered to one side and rammed its nose into a clump of bushes and deep snow, rendering it immobile.

Jack climbed out and wrestled with the tail while Michel gunned the motor, an action which only ploughed us deeper into the drift. They then told me to get out to lighten the load while Michel gunned the motor once more. The resulting back draught knocked me over and sent me flying over the snow where I landed face down, pinned by the force of the blast. If I had tried to get up I would have been blown right into the bushes.

The plane finally spun sideways. This diverted the back draught and allowed me to get up onto my feet and struggle to firmer ground. My nose had turned white and the plane was still stuck. Since it was obviously futile to wrestle with the plane any more in the bitter cold, Jack decided to go back to the village for help. He asked if I would like to go with him, but I didn't think I could make it. Instead I awkwardly tried to climb into the plane to get out of the wind before I froze to death, my gauntlet mitts giving me little grip in the bitter cold.

Somehow I managed it and curled up in the front seat, wrapped myself in my sleeping bag and shook, and shook, and shook. Whether it was from fright or cold or both I am not sure, but I just couldn't stop. Michel was still outside struggling with the plane when some men from the village appeared, all sympathy and assistance. With their help Michel extricated the plane from snow and bush and maneuvered it to firmer footing out on the ice at a reasonable distance from the trees. By this time Michel was so cold that both he and Jack had to return to the village to get warm, leaving me in the plane with the motor roaring and the propeller spinning. From my sleeping bag I stared at the rows of dials in front of me, at the spinning propeller and at the silent bush.

After what seemed an eternity they did return and in some wobbly fashion got us up in the air. I curled up on the luggage in the tail once more, still wrapped in my sleeping bag. It was too cold to check the thermometer, but my breath rolled in white clouds over the folds of the sleeping bag and swirled around in the draughts that came through the openings in the plane's fuselage.

Down below the country was silent and cold—hundreds of miles of empty snow dotted with little trees. But the weather did hold as the manager had predicted and, with the wind behind us, we made good time to Attawapiskat. There Father Pépin received us in the usual kindly fashion of the missions. Father ordered three lunches for us, but then looking at me said with a gentle smile, "Well, perhaps just two and a half."

After lunch it was back into the sleeping bag once more and up in the air. I could not see much except the grey sky and now and then a glimpse of empty landscape. Not having recovered from my earlier fright, every time the motor changed pace or the pilot clutched at the controls or the plane wobbled and stuttered, my heart sank. In this uncertain fashion we reached Moose Factory about 3:30, half the time it had taken to go north when we had been hampered by strong headwinds.

All that I had learned from the people of Winisk I recorded and would report to headquarters in Toronto. Included was my recommendation that the department buy the Lands and Forest house if it were available. Never in my wildest dreams did I imagine that I would one day spend an odd sort of honeymoon in that house and, later, the first three years of my married life.

LIFE ON THE BAY

■

When I finally joined George at Winisk in the fall of 1973, life settled into a more or less regular routine. Each day George went off to school at the far end of the village, while I did my best to clean and scrub and put together a lunch for him at noon and then some sort of dinner at night. My cooking was not the best, but I had a little set of cookbooks that I had at one time bought for my mother and another cookbook, produced by the Department for use in the North. It described how to cook goose and moose and skunk and other exotic dishes. It also had the standard recipe for bannock which I tried since it is a staple food of the north. However, the biscuits turned out like rocks which I threw out to the dogs that roamed the village, hoping that George would not know anything about them. But even the dogs refused to eat them.

When George came home at noon he announced with some puzzlement, "Say, there are a bunch of dogs running around out here holding their stomachs. What do you suppose is the matter with them?"

I burst into tears as the only reply I could think of.

George was amused by the ruined bannock, but outraged one time when I boiled some precious oranges. Both fresh fruit and vegetables were extremely rare. I had wanted to make the best use of these few oranges that came from somewhere in the south. My set of books had a recipe for boiled oranges which seemed like a good idea to me. George refused to eat them, although Father Daneau, who came to dinner each Sunday evening, said they were just fine. Unfortunately this was the way he described anything I cooked, no matter what it was or how inedible.

One night when he came through a wild blizzard, all we had was bacon and eggs with rice and bran muffins. Somehow the muffins had hard beans mixed in with them as the packages had burst in the mail and the contents mixed together. I don't know now why I did not sift the beans out of the mix, but perhaps I was not only lacking in culinary skills but in I.Q. too. Father still said they were fine. George wouldn't eat them.

When school was out, crowds of small children, predominately boys because there were far more boys than girls in the settlement, would roam in and out of the house. They would leaf through our magazines and books, sit on the carpet reading comic books and completing puzzles, and examine whatever objects of interest they found on our shelves. They always carefully replaced them where they found them. Never once did we lose anything, regardless of how attractive the item might be.

My journal of January 27/76 reads:

"Right now there are 11 boys in the house—3 Chookomoolins eating soup and the others reading and drawing. What a crowd! Dino makes 12."
"I mended Robert's jacket and George washed it."

If I left a cake on the kitchen counter, some small youngster might appear chewing on a handful that he had appropriated on his way through. If we left our plate of food on the table unattended for a few minutes, some small child might help himself to a forkful in our absence as he roamed about. Of course we would have been welcome to do the same in his house and that was understood.

Now and then George's brother, Carman, who lived on a farm in the south, would send us a box of apples. These, as all other shipments, came on the bi-monthly plane to the air base. Once there they were loaded onto snowmobiles or into canoes and transported across the river to the village. The apples would emit an enticing smell that brought the children into the house to share the bounty. One time Carman sent tomatoes which looked much like apples, but tasted vastly different and did not please the children at all.

Two little girls were in the house one day when some stalks of celery arrived. By that time I was washing vegetables in raw river water not knowing whether I was adding or subtracting germs by doing so. The girls had never seen celery before, but when I offered them a taste they chewed on it thoughtfully and finally determined that they liked it enough to ask for more.

One fall on our way back into Winisk, I brought a large package of popping corn. This intrigued a group of small boys who clustered around the stove and listened to the staccato sound of the corn hitting the lid and sides of the pan like buckshot. If I took off the lid and the popcorn leaped out into the air that was even better. With melted butter and salt sprinkled on the top, a potful went home to share with each family. The enthusiasm of the children for this intriguing operation was satisfaction enough for me.

Bread was a precious commodity in the village. Rubbery commercial loaves came into the store now and then, but home made bread was so much better. Since we had the only oven in the village, one youngster would come periodically to make bread for his family, and he made it well. Always wearing a round, crocheted hat with a tassel hanging down the side, he would mix and knead and let rise, then return later for the baking. In homes without ovens the village people had to rely on top of the stove dishes, chiefly pots of caribou or goose, or fish fried in the pan. Our oven became increasingly popular.

During George's first year at Winisk he thought he should introduce the people to growing potatoes to supplement their diet. Accordingly he ordered a sack of potatoes that were shipped, in at sixty-six cents a pound over the purchase price, and delivered to

Robert helps his mother by baking bread.

34

the school. With the help of the children, he dug a garden on the river bank then showed them how to cut each potato into a suitable chunk, with an eye showing in each.

One afternoon the children followed George up and down the rows, dropping a potato piece into each depression that they had made in the ground. When they were finished and the potatoes covered, the garden looked splendid and George regarded it with pride. The next morning on his way to school he again visited the potato patch only to find that, during the night, every piece of potato that had been so carefully planted the day before, had been dug up and appropriated.

"They did not miss one," he marvelled. Indeed, when he went into some of the houses he found the people happily frying his potatoes on top of the stove, some with bits of earth still attached.

"But, George," I reasoned, "You did not explain to the children that if the potatoes were left alone they would grow and multiply. No doubt the children very kindly agreed to help this mad white man who buried good food in the ground. He would never miss it if they dug it up again and put it to proper use."

It was George's last attempt the make farmers of them.

Another time when he was at Fort Severn, one-hundred and eighty kilometers west of Winisk, he ordered in a huge bunch of bananas just to let the children taste this fruit they had never seen before. The transportation cost alone was forty dollars.

Although the Hudson's Bay store stocked a variety of canned goods, food generally depended on the migration of both the caribou and the Canada geese.

My journal of April, 1973 reads:

"At present there is no meat in the village, the caribou being long gone and the wild geese not yet arrived although reports have come of sightings at Fort Albany and Attawapiskat farther south. Yesterday we had a tin of canned meat balls from the store, and today we bought a round can of Danish bacon for $1.25. We also have a can of tinned chicken legs sitting on the shelf and a can of corned beef hash (57 cents), all of which we will use sparingly. Instead we have been eating maccaroni and dried vegetables with which we make soup. We also have eggs left over from the supply George brought in at

Christmas (four months before), and a little bit of butter. Mostly the butter is tinned and has a peculiar rancid smell that permeates most of the cooking."

With some enthusiasm George brought home from the store a colourful little package of prepared breakfast cereals in individual boxes. I opened one box which contained something puffed and sugary and with the consistency of lead shot. Even with the powdered milk on it, it resisted all attempts of my teeth, strong though they be.

As with other leftovers I put it on the back porch for the dogs where it received the ultimate insult. The dog across the road, with the unlikely name of "Three," came tearing over as soon as the door opened, looking for a light snack of almost anything. She sniffed suspiciously at the cereal with its milk in the nice, white bowl, in itself an unusual feature of the usual canine dining, then gave me an offended look and walked away. And there it sat, the lead shot cereal, ignored and abandoned in an Indian village full of hungry dogs. The rest of the boxes contained what looked like snipped up cardboard, totally inedible by either humans or dogs.

At that point the village was also out of coffee. We had none and the store had none. We had lots of tea, but our fancy tended to dwell on visions of steak, and salad and steaming cups of coffee with lots of cream. Tea was nice, but somehow not quite the same, especially since we had no kettle in which to boil water, nor a tea pot in which to make tea. There were three good cooking pots in the house. If they were not being used to boil something, one was used for boiling water and one for making the tea, which could be quite good that way. That is, if you didn't mind the occasional bit of oatmeal or soup remnant in it and if you didn't mind a good portion of it sloshing onto your person as you poured.

To supplement the children's diet, the government provided the schools with dozens of boxes of rock hard, dry biscuits that you could hardly break with a hammer. Along with them came cartons of powdered milk. I discovered that at one time our house had boasted a meat grinder as one of its few kitchen utensils, but that George had taken it to school. Each day he would grind the biscuits into meal. Every morning before school he would mix this ground meal with the reconstituted milk, set the mixture on the space heater that warmed the classroom, and serve it at morning recess as porridge with a sprinkle of sugar on top. The children eagerly wolfed it down, as George himself did from time to time. The biscuits no doubt contained valuable vitamins and other nutrients, but this was the only way the children, whose teeth were generally not in good shape, could benefit from them. Advice regarding "*Canada's Food Rules*" that came into the school from time to time was greeted with the same bewilderment that many other directives from the south received.

Attendance at the school varied from about ten to twenty or more children, depending on when families went out onto the trapline or over to the goose camp in the fall. But children of all ages who remained in the village would drift into the school, even the tiny tots, too young to go to school. Often enough they fell asleep on the floor.

Ivan was one such youngster, a chubby boy of about three. When it came time for George and the others to come home for lunch, there lay Ivan sound asleep below the blackboards. Not wanting to wake him, George wrapped him in his own parka because of the bitter cold weather and carried him all the way to his home, which was across the trail from our own house. As he laid him on the bed, Ivan opened his dark eyes and grinned up at him, "Mona nepa (I wasn't asleep)," he said

"I could have strangled him," George declared, being half frozen without his parka in the icy wind.

On weekends George would take me out onto the flats and outcroppings of gravel that had arisen since the river receded at summer's end. The banks were grassy and overgrown with goose grass and willows. Behind them were the ponds and puddles where the wild geese loved to feed. George poked through pile after pile of rocks, finding one on which fossils were embedded and another with mica and granite and various other formations combined. I had no interest in these oddments, but still allowed George to fill the pockets of my jacket with samples, as his jacket had no pockets. Then we found an over-ripe goose egg stuck in the mud and this he tied into the hood of my parka for safe transport home.

Chief Alex's three dogs started out with us in the bright sunshine, enthusiastically chasing the yellow-legs, the sandpipers and the pigeons that skimmed over the water, impudently close. At one bend in the river the water rumbled over shallow rapids that sparkled and sang in the sun. Up the river from the rapids a band of sunlight led up to the sky. Geese rose and winged overhead and the tall grass swayed all around us.

I went on a hunting expedition with George only once. For four hours we wandered over the flats, towards the mouth of the Winisk River where it drains into Hudson Bay. We meandered through the marshy grasslands along the shore, making short treks out onto the gravelly shallows that rose here and there above the water. The rocks were mostly limestone with little to interest a geologist. The vegetation, though, was lush and green, waving briskly in the breeze. There were fields of white Arctic cotton and the jointed goose grass on which the geese fed. There were clumps of willow and high islands of spruce and poplar that swelled above the grass. In flood time the whole area would be under water with only the islands visible, but at that point the water was low and we could explore for miles over the river bed. Here and there lay pools and small lakes whose surface rippled in the wind. They would be the deep spots when the river was running fast.

Some miles downstream were wide, grassy meadows where the geese were settling in for the night. George and I crept into a clump of willows whose branches afforded a springy bed in which to rest. Not far away a flock of about sixty geese stood in the meadow, their necks raised in caution. They knew that we were there.

In a pasture a little farther along, another flock of about the same size grazed more confidently, knowing they were out of range. Now and then groups came in for a landing, their wings outspread and their feet reaching out from their bodies to make a neat landing. George crawled to a closer clump of bushes, but the geese took alarm and flew up in a flickering, white cloud.

We walked on further, creeping down a shield of driftwood as a small, new flock drew near. George fired with his shot gun and hit one that faltered and then began to sink to the earth below the rest of the geese as they headed westward. He drifted for some time till he sank to earth too far away for us to pursue him.

I thought about him all the way home. Was he all right? Could

Millie Hubbert outfitted in a traditional parka. Note the intricate hand-stitching on the garment.

he fly again? Did he have a mate who would support him or be bereaved? I began noticing the number of times a man in a hunting party would come in and say, "I've had enough. Hunting is over for me."

When Crown Attorney Burton was in he said, "I'll hunt no more. I get no thrill out of approaching a wounded goose that is sitting there waiting for the axe to fall." The Native people and the people of the North had to kill the geese for food, but I could not see how anyone could call it sport. Even George would rather watch the geese through his field glasses than shoot them. Often he declared that he missed them when he fired, as his heart was not in hitting them. I was not even enthused about eating geese after that trip for they seemed to have a musty, heavy taste that did not sit well on my stomach. I decided I would go on no more hunting expeditions.

39

On his own, however, George did continue to go out hunting, which usually resulted in few geese but a black and blue shoulder from the recoil of his shot gun. He had been using high powered Magnum shells which almost separated the shoulder muscles. Alex said that they were too powerful for geese because you could shoot a long way off with them, but you would lose the geese in the distance. Less powerful shells that dropped the geese closer by were more practical for the purpose of hunting.

Most mornings at five George would decide he wouldn't go hunting, but each evening he would make up a lunch in anticipation. Although it would have been improper for any of the men of the village to visit me while George was at work, some of the women, especially those who could speak English, would drop in from time to time to do a washing or to have a cup of tea. Two of the younger ladies were in one day, discussing a woman at the far end of the village whose children, they both agreed, bore a remarkable resemblance to a former Hudson's Bay manager.

I thought for a moment then asked: "Are there any children in the village with a particularly big nose and big feet?"

Without a trace of a smile one answered, "If there are, we wouldn't tell you."

I laughed as I repeated the conversation to George when he got home from school. He was not amused.

THE GREAT TOILET CAPER

Then there was the great 'toilet caper'. Since the Native people had neither electricity nor running water in their houses, they had outhouses at the back, or some sort of makeshift inside or just the wide outdoors. This presented a great difficulty to the old people, to those who were ill and those with small children and so on, to say nothing of the effluence that flowed from the yards into the river in the spring.

While I was in the south one summer, I noticed the house trailers that rolled along the highways and the many houseboats that travelled the waterways. They all had camp toilets that used two gallons of water mixed with a blue liquid that recycled for seventy-five flushes. After each flush you pumped more liquid back into the bowl. Why could they not be used in the Native houses?

I wrote a letter to one of the columnists in *The Globe and Mail* and the response was overwhelming. Camp toilets began arriving by the dozen. The first we took to Jacob Gull who was over eighty, confined to his bed and tended by his daughter, Alexandra who was not well either. The second we took to Jane Patrick, also well over eighty years old and not in good health at the time. We took one to Mike Patrick and his wife who lived in a tiny house with a tin stove in the middle, a big box of caribou meat in the corner and the floor covered with wood chips. Mrs.Patrick laughed heartily when we explained the use and operation of the toilet, but was happy to have it set up.

Cheques also came in. With this money we ordered as many toilets as the amount allowed. An official from the United Church phoned to ask how many toilets we wanted and, when I gave him a number, said he would see that we got them. An elderly woman wrote explaining that when she was young her mother used to put coal oil down the toilet so that it wouldn't smell.

Fifteen toilets came in in one shipment with a large supply of chemical called Liquid Gold. This I surmised was formaldehyde mixed with a blue colouring and some kind of perfume. Boxes and boxes of it came in, all of which we distributed to the houses.

The toilets were a great success, even with old James and Charlotte Mack. When a medical team came in one day, a Native girl was with them who spoke both English and Cree. She went around to the houses with us, making sure that the people really understood how the toilets operated.

The manufacturer of the toilets eventually became quite excited when he found out how these items were being used. He envisioned them installed in all Native houses in the north.

"We could make them up in a kit," he told us, "and we could call it a 'Millie Kit' and ship them all through the North."

I was noncommittal about the name, wondering if that would be my legacy to posterity, but delighted if the use of the toilets could be widespread. Name aside, I urged the manufacturer to approach the Indian Affairs office to see if they would purchase these toilets for use throughout the north. He did not have much success. This was a new idea and new ideas do not go well with bureaucrats.

The official attitude was much the same when I tried to persuade their builders to build outdoor privies for all the schools. This idea was greeted with jeers and derision. Instead all new schools were provided with indoor flush toilets and septic tanks. The first day of school some child was sure to drop something down the toilets and plug them up. With the nearest plumber hundreds of air miles away and unlikely to appear before freezeup, the whole plumbing system would be frozen solid and be unworkable. As a result the schools did without toilets until the following spring when a plumber might or might not arrive.

I tried to explain how the other institutions in the north handled the problem. The Mennonites, for instance, had a kind of indoor plumbing for night use or for those who were sick, but every school had a row of well kept privies outside for use at other times. It worked wonderfully well. However, Indian Affairs, organized from Ottawa, would learn from no one else, but continued to handicap the north with inappropriate urban practices.

In spite of officialdom, money and toilets continued to arrive at Winisk until I think every house in the village was supplied. A Susie Paulson, the mother of Lindy Loutitt, the pilot that I used to teach many years before at Moose Factory, came in on some government errand. She said she had been in one of the houses where they were pleased to tell her that they had an indoor toilet now. They had set it up in a corner behind a curtain and invited her to use it. Susie said she was too shy to use it with them sitting right there. "I didn't think I knew them that well." She laughed.

Publisher's Note

Millie Hubbert often chuckled over the possibility that she would be remembered as the person who popularized the use of portable toilets in Canada's north. But putting toilet humour aside, the author rightfully acknowledged the importance of her accomplishments which improved comfort and hygiene for countless native families.

Following Millie Hubbert's passing, I was given the opportunity to review the many files she left behind. Coming upon a particularly fat file folder labelled toilets, I was over-whelmed at the extent of the correspondence between Millie and countless sponsors of the portable toilets she promoted so successfully. A selection of the numerous letters exchanged between Millie and others are reproduced at this time. They speak volumes.

March 25, 1975

Dear Mrs. Hibbert,

I was interested in your appeal for money for chemical toilets for the people of your Indian village which appeared recently in the <u>Globe and Mail</u>. If the response follows the usual course you will probably be inundated with cheques and money orders from the people of Ontario and the rest of Canada.

If it works out that way, fine. If not, please write me (stamped, self-addressed envelope enclosed) and I shall send you my cheque for $100.00 to help your project.

I am a retired school teacher and have been a foster mother to four children in the Far East for many years. One of my regrets that it is impossible to do the same thing for Indian and Eskimo children. However there are many needy situations and if you get plenty of help from others I would rather use my $100.00 for one of them. If you don't get the necessary assistance, PLEASE do get in touch with me--say in a couple of weeks and I shall send the cheque by return mail.

Yours sincerely

Ellen Stevenson

(Miss Ellen Stevenson)

Mr. Donald MacLeod,
Toronto, Ontario.

Dear Mr. MacLeod;

Thank you so very much for the ten dollars you sent to help buy chemical toilets for the Indian people here at Winisk.

It is needed very badly, and with prices so high here it is difficult for the people to buy these things themselves.

The toilets are going to be a great blessing to the people and I would like to thank you most sincerely for your kindness on their behalf.

Yours truly,
Mrs. G.R. Hubbert

Winisk, via Moosonee, Ont. POL 2HO,
Telephone Winisk 34, Area Code 705,
April 8/75

Mr. D. Millar,
National Trust Co.,
Northtown Plaza,

Willowdale, Ontario.

Dear Mr. Millar:

I recently put a note in the Globe and Mail asking if
people would be interested in helping to supply toilets
for the Indian people here at Winisk.

We have had quite a response, and a number havve sent
me cheques with which to buy the toilets. I thought
that perhaps I should not mix this money with my own
but should establish a separate account for it. One
person wanted to know if I had established a fund that
she coulddsend an amount to directly, and I suppose
this is what she meant.

I am enclosing the cheques I have received to date,
totalling $384.62. I will be ordering the toilets
and paying for themffrom this amount. I would appreciate
your advice as to whether this is the best way to handle
the situation.

More money may very well be coming, but I have no idea
how much. It may be that I will be away from home and
down to the hospital in Moosonee for most of next week
but I should be back home on April 18th.

Sincerely,

Mrs. G.R. Hubbert

Canadian Red Cross Youth

TORONTO-CENTRAL BRANCH
460 JARVIS STREET, TORONTO 5
POSTAL CODE M4Y 2H5

923-6692

April 14, 1975

Mrs George Hubbert,
Winisk, Ontario

Dear Mrs Hubbert
    Your letter dated April 8th,1975,arrived to-day. I checked
the number of the enclosed statement with the one in the catalogue and found them to be the same,so the cheque you received
is definitely for the Pot Pourri.
    Your suggestionthat you order one toilet directly from San-
itation Equipment and pay for it with the refund,is a great
idea and will save going through a third party.
    As I told you on the phone last week, Mrs Jarvis Hunt sent
a cheque to us at Red Cross to be used to purchase two toilets
and a case of chemicals for Winisk. These will be ordered as soon
as her cheque comes through our accounting office.
    She also stated that she would like to help with some
smaller project as well. I suggest you write her and tell her
that you heard from me. She is very interested in the Native
people. Her address is 10 Avoca Ave. Toronto M4T 2B7
    I am so happy that the Christmas gifts are still keeping
the children cosy and warm and that so many of them have learned
to play the organ- thanks to the generous sharing of your time.
    With all good wishes to you, your husband and the children
of Winisk.

                Sincerely

                Madeline Ward
                Mrs. M. Ward

[handwritten note left margin] rec'd May 1'3

[handwritten note left margin] order # T 5065

[handwritten note] *bottle broken*

[handwritten P.S. bottom left] P.S. Please excuse all errors. Mary, my secretary is away on her holiday. I meant her honeymoon!!

46

Winisk, via Moosonee, Ont., POL 2HO,
May 21, 1975

Mr. Bruce Found,
Adam Scott Collegiate Vocational Inst.,
Peterborough, Ontario, K9H 5R6

Dear Mr. Found:

Thank you for your letter of May 7 and your offer of two toilets for the people of Winisk. We actually have enough now so that each family in the village has one, but we could probably do with a few spares for those who will need them in the future.

You mentioned visiting Winisk at some point. Please note that mail is very slow here and we just received your May 7 letter yesterday. I will be unable to mail this one, but we could probably do with a few spares for those who will need them in the future.

Towards the end of June the school closes, although we do not have the exact date yet. We will be leaving at that time, and immediately prior will be packing our belongings and getting ready for the summer. During the weekends in June not many people are in the village, including ourselves as most try to get away somewhere while the weather is fine. Plans are never very firm but this is the general trend.

If you wished to come during July or August, we would not be here, but you could probably get accommodation at the Ministry of Transport base where the planes land. The man in charge is Mr. Victor Fowke, M.T.C., Winisk, via Moosonee, Ontario (Telephone Winisk 33, Area Code 705).

You mentioned that Mr. McLennan is interested in having some of the Winisk children visit in the south before they go out to high school. Our school is very small, and we do not expect that any will be going out during the coming year as they are too young yet for high school.

Because the time is so short, it might be advisable to postpone your visit until the summer when you would have more time and when the weather might be more stable. For the past week it has been raining heavily and there has been little flying.

We appreciate very much your kind interest in the people of Winisk and hope that the foregoing may be useful.

Sincerely,
Mrs. G.R. Hubbert

P.S. Prior to your visit it would be in order to check with the chief at the same address as above.

Winisk, via Moosonee, Ont., POL 2HO,
Telephone Winisk 34, Area Code 705,
May 26, 1975

Mrs. Mary E. Shaw,
The Distaff Club,
Richmond Hill, Ontario,
L4C 3R7

Dear Mrs. Shaw:

Thank you so very much for the donation of fifty dollars towards the purchase of a toilet for the Indian people here at Winisk. We have almost enough to supply one to each family in the village, and with any surplus we are going to buy a supply of the chemical that goes with them.

The toilets are working wonderfully well and are a real blessing to the people, especially the old and the very young and those who are ill. In the spring there is a great deal of infection throughout the village, probably due to the refuse that melts and runs across the land and into the river. We are hoping that the toilets may help to cut down on this hazard and that the infection will be reduced next spring. The medical people are interested in seeing how the project turns out in case its application may be suitable for other settlements.

I was interested in seeing that your letter came from Richmond Hill. I used to teach there some years ago when my name was Millie Young. I taught in the main school on Yonge St. across from the movie theatre when Mrs. Walter Scott was principal. It was quite some time ago and I don't suppose anyone there remembers me now, but I had two very happy years there.

We do appreciate the thoughtfulness of the Distaff Club in being concerned about the welfare of the Indian people here at Winisk. Your gift means a great deal to the people and I thank you on their behalf.

Sincerely,
Mrs. G.R. Hubbert

Winisk, via Moosonee, Ont., POL 2HO,
Tel.Winisk 34, Area Code 705,
October 6/75,

Sanitation Equipment,
1080 Alness St.,
Downsview, Ontario,
M3J 2JI

Att: Mrs. Ferguson

Dear Mrs. Ferguson:

Thank you so much for the 737 model which arrived
safely in the last mail. It looks great and we are
trying to decide where would be the best place for it
and the best method of drainage. One thing, though,
the cap seems to be missing from the drain at the back
at the right side as you face the unit. It looks as
though it might be part # 522. The ring #542 is there
but that is all.

The new superintendent at Moose Factory seems to be
a particularly alert person and I will be sending him
the information about the project, hoping he might
get some installed in other settlements. The ones that
are here are working wonderfully well and the people
are so pleased with them.

Please thank Mr. Sherman for me too. We are very happy
with the whole project.

Sincerely,

Mrs. G.R. Hubbert

Winisk, via Moosonee, Ont., POL 2H0,
Tel. Winisk 34, Area Code 705,
October 6/75

Mr. D. Allen,
Dept. Indian Affairs,
Moose Factory, Ontario.

Dear Mr. Allen:

I thought you might be interested in the enclosed
information about the toilets which we got for the
Winisk people.

Each house now has a portable one (#707) and they are
working very well indeed. The company let us have them
for about $60.00 which is quite a reduction over the
catalogue price.

They have now sent us as a sample the model #737
which is a permanent installation emptied through
a valve in the bottom. The #707 has to be carried
out for emptying, although it is fairly light, and it
only has to be done about once a week.

Since they are working so well here we thought they
might be considered for other settlements, particularly
if the permanent model works as well as we think it
will. You might be interested in seeing them if you
get up to Winisk as we hope you will.

Sincerely,

Mrs. G.R. Hubbert

Sanitation Equipment Ltd.,
Downsview, Ontario M3J 1J1

Dear Millie:

Thank you for your letter and so happy you received the 737 Potpourri O.K.

The cap does not go on that unit—it is a permanent installation and therefore is supposed to be vented up to the roof or to the outside—however, we do not the the 1 1/2" vent pipe and are enclosing a plug that can go into the fitting already there.

Also, Millie, we are mailing to you today four cases of Liquid Gold— these are donated by Grace Church (United) Unit #7, Church Women, Brampton, Ontario—Mrs. Margaret Owen, 84 McCall Street, Brampton, Ontario was the lady who phoned, so hope we can get these to you before the mail strike.

October 10, 1975

Mrs. E. Ferguson

Winisk, via Moosonee, Ont., POL 2H0,
Feb. 14/76

Sanitation Equipment,

Downsview, Ont.,
M3J 2J1

Dear Mrs. Ferguson:

Would you please send us a hundred dollar order of the
Liquid Gold for the toilets.

The Superintendent from Moose Factory was up this week
and said that they had agreed to install the 737 model
in all the Indian houses on the coast here as a joint
venture between Indian Affairs and the Dept. of Health
and welfare. For some reason the Dept. of Health and
Welfare decided against it at the last moment, which is
really too bad.

The toilets are still doing well here. Not everybody
is using them, but enough are to prove their value. We
keep a supply of the liquid to give out to those who ask.

I am wondering what the people will do for Liquid Gold
when we leave as we are thinking of retirement in the near
future. I was counting on the people buying it from
Eaton's catalogue, but with the mail order service being
discontinued I don't know what they will do. Simpsons
doesn't seem to have it. Is there any way it could be
sold through the local store, or will Simpsons be stocking
it?

The extra pieces for repairing the units arrived in a later
mail.

March 3, 1976
Winisk, via Moosonee, Ont., POL 2HO,

Mr. C.S. Williams,
Orangeville, Ontario,
L9W 1A7

Dear Mr. Williams:

I am pleased to sign the enclosed receipt for the gift of one
hundred dollars that you so very kindly sent for the Indian
people of Winisk. You will be pleased to know that the
toilets continue to work very well, and we have been able to
provide a continuing supply of the liquid for them. zxz
(A little Indian baby is staying with me just now while his
mother is in hospital and he just began to hit the keys of the
typewriter when I was not looking).

I am not sure whether the Income Tax people will accept
the receipt of a private person but you can try and see what
they say. We are not a Mission here, but my husband teaches
at a federal school for Indian children of the village. With
your kind help and that of other people in the south we
have been able to provide a few extra things that make such
a difference to those who have so little.

You might be interested in knowing that we have bought a
farm at Markdale, not too far north of you, and will be
retiring there sometime in the near future.

Thank you for your help in assisting with the project here at
Winisk.

Sincerely,
Mrs. G.R. Hubbert

A CELEBRITY ARRIVES

—————— ▪ ——————

"Edgar Bergen's come to visit!"[2] It was our friend Albert at the door, with the party of hunters he was guiding while they were at the goose camp across the river. Every fall as soon as the goose season opened, most of the villagers closed their houses and moved across the river to the abandoned air base where a number of the buildings had been retained as a camp. This camp was mostly for Americans who came up each year to shoot geese, although the number of geese that were actually shot was minimal. The air base had been part of the Mid-Canada Line, one of the chain of radar stations built and manned by Canadians stretching along the 55th parallel from Labrador to British Columbia.

We had heard that Edgar Bergen woul be coming to the camp this year and wondered if he would bring Charlie McCarthy with him. Such a guest would be of great interest to the children. I opened the door and in they all walked, Edgar Bergen, along with a number of his friends from Hollywood, and our friend Albert. Charlie McCarthy was not in the group, but was back in camp apparently resting.

Albert was delighted to introduce us to the party, then set about making coffee for everyone. Albert was familiar with our kitchen especially when he was going out on the trapline. In he would come and open each cupboard door.

"Can I take this?" he would ask, holding up some item of food. If I said "Yes" he would put it in his packsack then search for something else. "Take this?" If I said "No" he would put it back on the shelf without rancour and search further. Eventually he would have a small bundle of canned and packaged food to add to his supply for the trapline. We were happy to accommodate him for it in no way inconvenienced us.

And now here he was, making coffee for Edgar Bergen and his friends who were ranging about the room in their "hunting clothes," items that they would undoubtedly never wear again. I was happy to have them, but somewhat disconcerted because just a few days earlier we had received a new washing machine. Getting carried away with the luxury of the thing, I had washed nearly everything in the house and draped them wherever I could attach a clothes line. In front of the sunny, living room window was a particularly cosy spot. Normally I would have hung the clothes outside. But since the weather was inclement and I couldn't wait to try the new machine, the house was one vast clothes dryer.

I looked at all these Hollywood types and tried to picture the houses they probably lived in, complete with swimming pools and other luxuries, and wished I could retrieve at least the items of underwear that were hanging above their heads. But they were delightful visitors, enjoying the coffee, relaxing with Edgar telling jokes as the life of the party. When they had finished, they all signed my guest book. Albert led them down the trail to meet George and the children in the school, however, since most most of the children were over at the goose camp, the school was somewhat empty.

Edgar did bring a Charlie McCarthy doll to the camp and, some time before he left, he put on a show for the children. He no doubt had quite a number of these dolls, but after the concert sent this one over to the school for the children to keep. However, the children did not think that Charlie, with his top hat and tails, was dressed properly for the north. They therefore persuaded their mothers to make a pair of jeans and a bush shirt for him, with a kerchief around his neck and a pair of small beaded moccasins for his feet. Sitting up beside the blackboard, Charlie now looked much more comfortable attired in his new clothes in his northern surroundings. Eventually we took a picture of Charlie in his dashing outfit and sent it to Edgar, who returned a very appreciative letter with a photo of himself and all his famous dolls.

The new washing machine was a marvel to look at but, apparently because there was not enough water pressure to operate it, the clothes often came out of it looking worse than before they went in. Before its arrival I had washed in an ancient apparatus whose wringer did not work. This meant that I had to wring the clothes by hand. Conditions often meant that all colours went together and since George favoured blue shirts, I soon found that all my underwear had turned blue. Even though the winter sunshine was bright, the weather could be deceptively cold, often down to forty below and colder. George undertook to hang out the wash in that temperature, but, of course, everything soon was frozen stiff. Clothes tended to snap and crack if you tried to pry them off the clothesline.

Alex was in one time when we had just washed and he smiled, "It is easy to see that there is a woman in the house," he said, "because there is a washing on the line." I told Alex that all the time George had given me the impression that he produced a washing like that every week. Alex just smiled.

Because of the scarcity of water which had to be carried up from the river or derived from melted snow, the women of the village had a much more difficult time with washing than I did. Usually they would build a fire of willow branches inside a small teepee where they would set a wash tub full of water. When the water boiled they washed their clothes, then hung them on the clothesline to rinse and bleach in the sun and rain. It was a system that worked very well. Often the flapping clothes were the only indication of the direction of the wind to guide the pilots as they navigated their planes into the settlement. These clothes served more than one useful purpose.

When the goose camp was going full swing the village appeared deserted. The school could be so bereft of pupils that George often would close up until the season was over. That fall he, expecting to have spare time, had brought a snowmobile in with him, along with a set of snowshoes for me. The Native people had made his snowshoes extra long because of his height some years previously. George was particularly proud of the snowmobile and kept it in the livingroom for several months, apparently not wanting to take it outside and get it dirty.

Eventually George decided to make a little house for the skidoo near the back door. He started the project bravely enough until Father pointed out that if he drove the machine into the hut, he would have a terrible time trying to drag it back out again since the far wall was immobile against the back porch. The Native people knew this, but none would interfere in what another was doing, no matter how bizarre the efforts. George, therefore, dismantled the hut and started over again, planning a door both front and back so he could drive right through. With nearly everybody over the river, he was free to roam around the village, appropriating all the bits and pieces of lumber, plywood, boards, sidings and two-by-fours he could scrounge. He threw them together with reckless abandon.

George was certainly not a builder, so neither were the walls of the hut plumb nor the building square. At one point he got me to help by jumping on a two-by-four poised under a block of wood, that in turn would hoist a piece of plywood into the air where George would wham it with hammer and nails. I knew nothing of building, but did conjecture privately that this was no way to build a hut or anything else. But we had only been married a short while, so how could I be critical?

Part of the building was up, when he decided 'for a change of pace' to paint the portion he had finished. His purpose, he said, was to make sure that when the people came back from the goose camp, nobody could identify the pieces of lumber and what-not that he had stolen. For this job he used the same grey paint with which we had painted the bookshelves in the livingroom. It came from a bucket marked 'pump house,' but since nobody seemed interested in painting the pump house, we felt we could put it to a better use. Actually with the paint covering a multitude of errors, the shed began to look quite serviceable.

However, when the job was finished and the snowmobile in place, the first snowstorm filled the shed with snow packed so hard that George had to pry the machine out with scoop and shovel. From then on the hut remained empty while the snowmobile sat outside like all the other machines in the village.

Around that time another group of Americans came over from the goose camp, all dressed in their camouflage outfits with peaked caps and waist-high waders. This group was from South Carolina, one of them a prominent contractor who just had to go around to see the skidoo hut as he had no idea what it was. He regarded the structure with some wonder and said he had never seen anything quite like it. He then had to take pictures of George hammering away and of me standing in my cut off ragged at the knees jeans, ready to jump on whatever piece of plywood George might indicate.

"It would never pass muster in South Carolina," was the contractor's estimation. George didn't care. It suited him fine.

57

One day four Americans, unrelated to the goose camp, arrived in front of the house, having paddled for twelve days down the Winisk River from Webequi. All the young men had a two-week growth of beard. One of them, Philip, was a real estate agent and the other called Mike, was a historical writer for the American government. Bob was an architect and his wife, Anne, a supervisor of Day Care Centres in Michigan. Anne was tall and sturdy, of Swedish descent, with long, blonde hair and a ready laugh.

The party arrived with both an aluminum canoe and a plastic one filled with the best of gear to cope with any emergency that might arise. Philip said he and Mike had upset their canoe in rapids a few years earlier on the Rupert River on the other side of the Bay. They had spent five days wandering around the wilderness without any food. From then on they made sure they were prepared with flotation jackets, waterproof blankets and emergency kits as well as all the latest in survival gear.

They stayed with Father Daneau over night, but George invited them for a goose dinner at our house at noon on Saturday. While they were having dinner with us, a flock of geese flew over the house. George grabbed his gun, rushed out and took a few shots at them. Of course he missed, but the Americans were delighted. Philip said that he belonged to a group of men in the United States who were avid hunters and he couldn't wait to "lay this one on them."

The next day, Sunday, Bob borrowed George's shot gun and went hunting with one of the men of the village. When we came back from church we found a goose left in our porch, the results of his efforts. Late that night George plucked and cleaned it, then woke me up from a sound sleep to tell me it only took him nine minutes to do the job. I couldn't have cared less.

The American party had tried to radio out to Nakina for a plane to pick them up and fly them back to where their car and some friends were waiting. However, neither Father Daneau's radio was working because of a battery problem nor was the Hudson's Bay Company radio working because of weather conditions. But somehow the men managed to get their message out, summoning a single engine Otter with two pilots from Nakina. Since it was the first time either of the pilots had been to Winisk, they were very careful about their landing in the river among the shallows and rocks.

Following dinner of left-over goose with us, the pilots then strapped the two canoes to the pontoons of the plane and tried to take off. It wasn't easy because of the shallow water, the strong current and the stiff wind. George and I and a couple of men from the village held guy ropes on the pontoons till the plane moved away from the shore and drifted out into mid stream. The pilot taxied up river as far as he dared go, then drifted back as far as he dared drift to give him a long runway. He then gunned the motor and took off. Although heavily loaded, the plane rose from the river and disappeared over the bush.

The previous week, in the midst of wind and cloudy weather, the Hudson's Bay Company plane arrived with the District Inspector on board. The pilot, not knowing what the weather was like at Winisk as he was unable to contact us by radio, took a chance on coming anyway. They were about half way when the weather closed in with wind and rain and low hanging clouds, no weather for a small Beaver. The drone of the motor came through the wind, bringing the village people out open mouthed, to see the little plane sink slowly down through the clouds and gingerly approach the village. It came in slowly and carefully, almost putting down one toe at a time to touch the waves before settling in. Just as it did so, a gust of wind caught the wings, gave them a last angry shake and then let go. Everyone breathed again as the machine came to rest, still trying to maintain its equilibrium against the wind and current. It took some time before it could be manoeuvred up against the dock and the manager and all his goods hauled ashore.

The District Inspector, Mr. Howel, was a gracious, English gentleman dressed in a business suit and overcoat, apparently his idea of proper apparel for supervising in the North. So-dressed he sloshed up through the mud with the help of the Hudson's Bay Company manager and a few helpers.

Before long two boys appeared at our door with a big cooler of meat. "For George," they said with a twinkle in their eyes. I peeked in and was quite overcome by the quality and quantity of the gift. Then I realized that the meat "for George" really belonged to the Hudson's Bay Company to be stored in our freezer, the only one in the village. The price on the box of meat was $108.00.

My journal of Sept. 16, 1973 reads:

"Nobody in the village but us and the priest have a refriger-
ator so quite a number of people now have geese stored in
our refrigerators and deep freeze. The problem is that our
new generator has broken down again and we are operating
on Father Daneau's 3 kw. generator which does not generate
enough power for all the appliances. Last night the freezer
flickered and went out, but today it is operating once more.
Our electric freezer is stuffed with Susan's geese and the deep
freeze has H.B.C. geese and a box of Alex's geese along with
a few things of our own—a few cuts of 'outside' meat, some
loaves of store bread and the last of the butter we brought in
with us. The propane fridge has a very tiny freezer compartment and it is full too. We just hope the small generator will
continue to produce enough juice to keep it all going."

"The water pump is giving some distressing sounds again
and gasps and wheezes when it is turned on. Because of the
small generator we have to turn on the pump each time we
want to turn on the tap, then turn off the pump as soon as the
toilet is flushed or the sink filled with water. We keep a pail
of drinking water on the counter purified with halazone but
tablets are running out."

Before freezeup closed us in I tried to make some order out of
our motley collection of beds and mattresses. Since we had two
thirty-nine inch mattresses which for years had been lying on the
floor, I put in an order for two thirty-nine inch box springs. What
arrived was one fifty-two inch box spring and two extra twenty-
nine inch mattresses which made for a very curious arrangement.

Each afternoon I would go down to the school and walk George
home, often dropping into some of the houses as we passed. In one
house an older man was quite ill, lying on some sort of cot, attended to by a son and daughter-in-law. He sat up wheezing when he
saw us, his one bright eye alert. With much gusto he told stories of
how he used to travel by dog team to Fort Severn and even to York
Factory and Churchill. When we asked how he lost his eye, he said
the doctor took it out in a hospital in Winnipeg. George noted
that the mattress on which the man was lying was in very poor

George Hubbert ouside a smoke tent used for preserving game.

Food and equipment are stored in a cache out of the reach of the dogs.

shape. He eased our sleeping combination problem by taking one of the new twenty-nine inch mattresses down to the old fellow, carrying it on his back when he returned to school the next day.

Often after school George would take me for a walk down the river to where he knew many red currants were growing. The bank was overgrown with small trees until it dropped to the water in low marshy grasslands, green and lush. This day was warm except for the sharp wind that blew once you were out of the bush and on the open shore. Wild roses grew along with asters and fire weed, curled dock and horse tails and Labrador tea. Many varieties of willows prospered in clumps, along with chalk-white poplars with trembling leaves. In the bush were cranberries and strawberries in their season, but at that point the red and black currants were lustrously ripe. The problem was that as soon as you disturbed the bushes, the mosquitoes and black flies rose in clouds to gorge on any exposed skin, particularly that found around the hair line and the neck. Indian girls wore their hair hanging loose over their faces, which seemed to be one protection against the flies. I loosened mine and swished it around like a horse's tail, but still received a red band of beaded swellings around my head from insect bites. My hair, being short and curly, was not at all suitable for chasing mosquitoes.

Still, the berries were ripe and good. Among the red currants were tempting larger red berries which I was picking with enthusiasm until George pointed out that they were snake berries and supposedly poisonous.

On the way back home we wandered out onto the river shallows where the shore birds were hopping and splashing. George, ever careless of his comfort, safety or health, sloshed out over his boot tops from shoal to shoal and took a big drink of water directly from the river. This was downstream from the village where all the refuse and debris collected. Later George would develope slight diarrhoea which I maintained was from the river water.

One of the men from the village passed us with a pack full of blueberries. He had been out hunting geese, but seeing none had spent his time picking. At home the children were concerned when we showed them the red currants that we had gathered and said that only the bears ate them. Still I trusted that George had picked out all the offensive snake berries and that we could safely eat the rest. Actually, if the bears ate the berries I would now expect that they would be perfectly safe for us, but I did not think of that at the time.

When George was in school I now and then went for a walk by myself to the end of the village, where the little cemetery was waist deep in grass, and overgrown with bushes. A few white crosses stretched up through the growth, leaning every which way inside the broken fence. The last grave of the new infant was marked with a stake until the father would be able to replace it with a cross.

Somewhere beyond the cemetery was an old trail leading into the bush, but I tramped through the underbrush unable to find it. At the last house an old lady was hanging out clothes beside a line full of geese, all dead and hanging by their necks. I tried to ask her if I could take a picture of the geese. She smiled and, pulling her jacket around her, stood underneath them so I could capture both her and the geese with my camera.

In the yard stood a teepee which I thought was for smoking geese. When I motioned to it, she made scrubbing motions with her hands, then pulled aside the tent flap so I could see inside. There was a small spruce fire on the ground and a big wash tub filled with water, a scrub board on it and some clothes in the process of washing.

I then asked her where the path was that led into the bush and she went with me to show me. We walked down through the meadow and over a swift little stream which we had to leap, then up through the bush beyond. Hospitably she came with me all the way, pointing out the higher ground where I could step without sinking to my knees in the muskeg. When I thought we had gone far enough we turned around, and this time she showed me where a short log stretched over the stream so we could cross more easily. She hopped nimbly over, but had to turn and laughingly take my hand while I crossed. She went with me right down to the main road, then waved and went in to the nearest house when she saw I was safely on my way.

The next day George went to visit the little lady who had helped me find my way at the end of the village. Seeing that she too needed a new mattress, he told her husband that we had a mattress he could have. The old fellow came hurrying down to the house the next day at noon and trotted off with the other thirty-nine inch mattress. That still left us with two old thirty-nine inch mattresses and one fifty-two inch box spring.

The weeks leading up to freezeup were a busy time with our front window framing a constantly changing scene of life in the North. One day I thought a helicopter was coming right through the window, but it veered sharply at the last minute and put down daintily in front of the Hudson's Bay Company beside the flag pole. It was the RCMP patrol visiting all the goose camps now that the goose season had opened.

Before we heard the plane, several Native women hurried up to the front door to tell us that police were on their way and for George to hide his rifles or any geese that he might have shot without a licence. They expressed their concern for our welfare and watched anxiously to see if we would take their advice. George did.

One day the yellow Lands and Forest plane flew in and anchored below the bank with only its high tail visible from above. Five men, including the Ontario coroner and the Crown Attorney from Kenora, slogged up with all their gear to the tiny house which Lands and Forests still owned, next door to ours. The men were togged out in waders, jackets, vests and sweaters intended as protection against the sharp wind that was blowing. Although the day was bright, the thermometer outside the window read forty-four degrees Fahrenheit.

Before winter closed in another visitor arrived with Sam Edwards, a young East Indian man who wanted to marry Luke's young sister who was at that time about twelve years old. The visitor had never met her, but declared that he would wait until she was of age. However, he wanted to finalize the arrangements on the spot. He emptied his pockets onto our kitchen table, saying that would give the family all that he had with him and would arrange to send more when he got home.

Since he asked our advice we tried to explain that it was not possible in this country to, in effect, "buy" a wife. If he wanted to marry the girl he should come back at some later date to determine how both he and she felt at that time. I think that what finally dissuaded him was our comment that no matter what arrangements he made now, when he returned a number of years later the girl might or might not be available.

He put his current wealth back into his pocket and left, totally dissatisfied with the customs of this country and the North.

THAT'S ENTERTAINMENT

—————— ▨ ——————

Freezeup might take anywhere from two to six weeks. We would wait, often impatiently, for the river to freeze over sufficiently to allow the men and snowmobiles to cross. During that time there was no mail nor other supplies as nobody could get across to meet the plane.

One October the men made one last trip across the river to meet the plane, but they were afraid they might not get back to the village before nightfall. By that time the patches of ice that had been floating down stream for days piled up around the dock at the far side. They could not get their canoes from the bank to the open water. Along with mail and groceries and other sundries, on board the plane were a number of women with new babies, coming back from the hospital at Moose Factory and hoping to reach home before freezeup.

Eventually the men took the women and children and a couple of canoes up stream by a Bombardier to a place beyond the ice where they expected they could get their canoes into the water. If that were successful they would go back to the base and transport the mail and other goods the same way. After several cold and harrowing hours both canoes arrived back at the village with their loads, but it was the last crossing of the river until freezeup was complete.

When winter did settle in it was like hunkering down in a deep freeze with small boxes of warmth lining the trail. People hurried from one box to the next, all muffled in heavy parkas with fur trimmed hoods, with moosehide mitts attached to bright mitten strings, and all wearing duffle lined moccasins or heavy boots. Night closed in early through those long months while daylight came late. There was little in the village to offer for amusement, but the daily chores of cooking, cleaning and keeping warm kept most of us sufficiently occupied to fill the hours.

At the school George ordered movies from the National Film Board for the children and, if they were of sufficient interest, showed them to the villagers in the evenings. One of the first such movies I saw there was called "The Drylanders," a gloomy story I thought, but the people seemed to enjoy it immensely. They laughed heartily at the most unlikely places, such as when the old man of the family fell down in the field and had to be carried bodily into the house to die. This appeared to be the moment of highest amusement, although I could not see it.

The classroom was small and crowded to the door with people sitting on desks and chairs and on window ledges to see the films. With most of the adults smoking, it was a fire marshall's nightmare. Soon it became unbearably hot, especially since everyone was bundled up in skidoo suits, parkas and moccasins, all of which were too cumbersome to remove. There were three reels to this particular film. During the reel changes when the lights went on, the door was opened a fraction to allow a flow of icy air to billow into the stifling atmosphere. But when the picture again flashed onto the screen we all forgot about the heat and settled back to enjoy the story.

One time George was delighted to receive a set of four reels called "Below Zero" from the National Film Board. According to the description, they portrayed how the countries around the North Pole coped with frigid weather. Usually he reviewed all the reels in the school before showing them to the village, but he thought this such an excellent series that he publicized it widely after seeing only the first reel. He even gave a special invitation to Father Daneau as he always did when he had a particularly good film.

I thought the whole thing terribly boring as I watched scene after scene of bulldozers and heavy duty equipment and steam engines doing dear knows what in misty landscapes. Then the movie turned to Finland where the people survived by means of sauna baths. To our astonishment the camera abruptly swept us into one of those baths where a bevy of buxom ladies were all lolling about in the altogether, lazing in the steam which concealed absolutely nothing. While we were trying to grasp what we were actually looking at, the ladies came bouncing out of the sauna totally in the buff, dancing around the trees and tossing snowballs at one another.

Through this rather lengthy sequence the audience sat in stunned silence, then was just as suddenly whisked back to the heavy duty equipment and the bulldozers. There we sat in our parkas and mittens, mute with shock. George was furious! What had the National Film Board done? What did it mean by sending him movies of this nature? He would write to his Member of Parliament. He would see that justice was done! He was painfully aware that Father Daneau was sitting demurely in the front row at his special invitation, but the priest's only comment when the show was over was a quiet, "Very nice movie, George."

None of the other people said a word as they filed out, except for one young fellow who murmured as he left, "Say, George, you should get more movies like that," and his dark eyes twinkled. George was furious. Every time he saw George after that the same fellow would make some remark about, "You remember that movie you once showed about the North, George? That was really a good one." Then he would enjoy George's utter chagrin.

Sometimes Father would order movies which nearly everyone attended although, of course, they were all in English and the basic language of the entire village was Cree. Alex and his wife never went to these movies so his boys often went with us, Ivan or Danion holding tightly to my hand and trying to pace their short steps to George's long strides. One movie was an early Shirley Temple film made when she was about four years old. It was accompanied by a newsreel showing "The Highlights of 1939" with King George VI and Queen Elizabeth visiting the United States, President Roosevelt opening the World's Fair and the Russians bombing Helsinki, all of course in black and white. There was also a cowboy movie with the good guys dressed in white and the bad guys in black, just the way it should be. All of us found the presentation very satisfactory, with no nude scenes or startling interruptions. Once by chance the Red Cross sent in the movie "Oliver Twist," an unexpected but welcome treat.

One of the men from the village began ordering commercial films of one kind and another for which he had to charge in order to cover the costs. He showed his movies in the old community hall which was a lot larger than the classroom, but bone chilling cold in spite of the barrel stove with which he tried to warm it. Sometimes it would be so cold that we would all have to huddle around the barrel stove in our parkas and mitts to try to keep warm, all the while listening to the howl of the storm outside. The uncomfortable furnishings of backless benches on plank flooring did not add to our comfort level.

His first film was an ordinary cowboy film which I thought not very interesting. The second was a rodeo movie with a lot of profanity and some sexy scenes to which George took great exception. He would have stamped out in protest if I hadn't stopped him. Once, however, he actually received "The Bridge on the River Kwai" which he showed four times before sending it back.

During breakup and freezeup when no one could cross the river to meet the plane, the village brought out three old movies that it had saved from some distant past. One was a movie about the war featuring a young Jack Hawkins, a favourite of George's since he had first seen it when it was shown to his regiment overseas. My favourite was a cowboy movie even though both the beginning and the ending were missing. Someone had tried to splice broken sections of the film together, but did not get them in the right sequence, creating a bit of confusion. However nobody cared. These movies had been shown so many times that most of the audience had internalized large portions of the dialogue, even though few of them spoke English.

"Are you having a good time, Mr. Winters?" some youngster would call out and a moment later the character on the screen would echo, "Are you having a good time, Mr. Winters?"

The doctor in the movie had a rather convoluted speech after examining one of the bodies that were scattered about the corral: "My preliminary examination was superficial. It looked like suicide. But it is a well established fact that no left handed man could shoot himself in the right temple." George concluded that extensive experiments must have been conducted, with right handed men shooting themselves in the left temple, and left handed men shooting themselves in the right temple until it was finally established that it couldn't be done. In any case nearly every small child in the audience could recite the comment verbatim, even though their basic language was Cree. Since the ending of the movie was long since gone we could only conjecture how it ended, but since most of them turned out the same way we could easily guess. When other movies were non existent, these old ones were endless favourites.

On the way home from the movies, our feet crunching in the ice-dry snow, the night sky would often be filled with a yellow-green curtain that waved above us in endless folds from one horizon to the other, lighting the trail, the tiny houses and the silent bush that wrapped us round. We would walk below this astonishing wonder in silence, watching wave after wave of light that illuminated our path and our whole world, and ultimately led us home.

Books were a precious commodity and much valued by the children.

A GHOST OF THE FAR NORTH

One of George's weekend diversions was to take his skidoo across the frozen river to the abandoned air base and rummage among its deserted buildings. The base had once been a part of the Mid Canada Line, a chain of radar bases built along the 55th parallel and operated by Canadians from Labrador to British Columbia. Work on the line began in late 1954.

Most of the materials and equipment were brought in by sea from Hudson Strait or from the railhead at Moosonee during 1955-56. Because of the shallow coastal waters, freighters anchored eight to ten miles offshore to unload onto barges which ferried the cargo to land. During that winter tractor trains from Moosonee assisted in the operation. They left tracks in the fragile muskeg still visible years later when the snow receded. In 1956 the population of Winisk was expanded by the seven-hundred labourers who helped build this major defence complex, due for completion in 1957. In January 1958, when all sites on the line became operational, the population at Winisk shrank to one hundred and fifty-nine.

In 1965 the whole system was closed down when improvements to the Pine Tree system located farther south made the Mid Canada Line no longer necessary. The control station at Winisk was one of the last to close, although the air strip-hanger complex continued to be used regularly by commercial and private aircraft.[3]

George found these derelict buildings fascinating. I went with him once or twice, but took a strong aversion to the place. The temperature both inside and outside was the same, far below zero. The walls of many of the buildings glittered with frost and the floors were deep in snow drifts that had blown in through broken windows. The chill went right through me and seemed to freeze my very soul.

Everywhere were traces of the comparative grandeur that once flourished in this remote outpost. There was a library from which most of the books had been purloined to light the Native fires.

71

There was an Olympic size gymnasium whose hardwood floor was still painted with the lines for basketball, volleyball and other games that had not seen players for years. In more recent time local people had found the place ideal for servicing their snowmobiles.

The kitchen was massive with a walk-in freezer, stainless steel stove, multiple sinks and rows of shelves and cupboards for storing dishes and food, all long since gone. On the floor of the dining room, almost buried in the snow, lay a menu with a red tassel attached, featuring the courses for the last Christmas dinner that was served there. It listed shrimp cocktail and turkey and all that goes with the traditional bird, along with suitable wines, plum pudding and coffee.

There was a large water filtration plant surrounded by bottles of chemicals of bewildering varieties. George thought he should remove and dispose of those marked 'sulphuric acid' and the like, but amused the children in school with the bottles of mercury which formed tiny, glistening balls that coalesced and rolled around the floor. There were dozens of bottles of other chemicals, most of which were totally unknown to me.

There was a store room still filled with piles of letter head notepaper and envelopes that George from time to time, would appropriate for the school. There were dozens of boxes of Brasso and Silvo meant for some mysterious and probably compulsory polishing. I took a few tins home, but couldn't find anything to polish in our environs in the village. We found a heavy, oak desk in one of the offices which George hoisted onto the back of the sleigh and transported across the river for Father to use in the Mission.

In the garages stood derelict vehicles of all descriptions— trucks, jeeps, a fire engine and a bus from whose windows I could envision ghostly faces peering out at me in disapproval. I couldn't wait to flee from the eerie atmosphere, feeling that an icy finger was about to descend on my shoulder at any moment.

The focus of the establishment was the Command Centre which featured an enormous map of the region, studded with tiny lights controlled by a keyboard that had not set them alight in many years. The snow on the floor was mixed with papers and booklets and other unidentifiable debris through which you had to scuffle to make your way. The hallways leading to the Command

Top. The ghost of the north. An abandoned radar building.
Left. Some of the equipment found in the remains of the Command Centre.

Centre were lined with tier after tier of radio equipment, serving some unknown purpose of long ago.

I hated the base, the unrelenting cold and the eerie feeling that we were not alone. George loved it. On his many trips he collected a vast pile of motors, bells and wires. These were placed all around the livingroom and joined together with long frayed cords, the last one plugged into one of our few electric outlets. When they were set in motion, wheels spun, lights flashed and bells rang serving no useful purpose whatever. George and the children, however, thought the performance was wonderful. I stepped gingerly over the electric conglomerate and pretended it was not there.

A particular fetish of George's was the fire alarm bells that were fastened to the outside walls of the base. Countless numbers of these he unscrewed and brought home. Eventually he parcelled them up and mailed them to his brother in the south. We never did find a use for them. Much better were the outside lights that he also packed and shipped out. As a result both the house and the barn of our first farm were well outfitted with them, as was the house I later had built in town. They look grey and utilitarian but with globes of glass something like one inch thick, they are virtually indestructible. I am very grateful for them though I never dreamed I would be.

When we were at the base we sometimes called in to the hanger to visit with the caretaker and the Native couple who maintained the complex. Now and then visitors from outside would be there, having dropped off a plane on some northern errand. Often they brought their own food with them. We would try not to gaze longingly at the steaks, lettuce, tomatoes and other fresh food they were putting in their mouths. We were doing the best we could on goose and rancid butter in the village. Food does merit special attention, particularly if one is deprived for a time.

Once, over freezeup, we were six weeks without salt, a situation which puts a premium on that commodity. I knew Father had salt at the Mission, but would not let him know our discomfiture because he would no doubt have given us the last that he had. I did not want him to do that. We just survived without salt since the store had none either.

No matter the season, the abandoned base was too much of a ghost for me. Often I was more content to remain in the village and wonder what George would bring back this time.

CALAMITY AND RESCUE

—————— ▦ ——————

For many years the Hudson's Bay Company annually replenished the supplies at its seven stores on James Bay—Rupert's House, East Main, Paint Hills and Fort George on the east coast, plus Kashechewan and Fort Albany on the west coast along with Winisk and Fort Severn on Hudson Bay. Normally the supply barges wintered at Paint Hills. When the waters opened up in the summer, they were towed down to Moosonee where the barges were loaded with goods that had come by railway from the south. When they were ready, tugs towed them along the coasts to the eagerly waiting settlements. The barges would then return to Moosonee empty for immediate reloading. In the early days this replenishment was the settlements' only contact with the outside world. After a long winter of almost complete isolation, the barge and its contents were greeted with celebration.

On September 22, 1972, the tug MV *Churchill River* with Barge 1001 in tow heading to Fort Severn, had reached a position thirty miles west and twelve miles offshore from Cape Henrietta Maria. There they encountered gale force winds estimated at sixty m.p.h. At 4:00 a.m., with no visibility, the bridle of the barge parted and the barge sailed before the wind towards the shore. The seas were running too high for the *Churchill River* to go alongside to pick up the safety line. With the shallow waters near shore rapidly approaching, the tug was obliged to move back out to sea and seek shelter in James Bay. When word of the disaster reached Winnipeg, a Hudson's Bay Company aircraft was despatched to search for the barge they eventually located some twenty-eight miles off Cape Henrietta Maria. It had been driven ashore so hard, by a combination of the tide and gale force winds, that it was left imbedded in the mud and rocks well above the high water mark.

All sorts of salvage experts made suggestions for recovery of the barge the cost of recommendations all having to be weighed against the value of its contents. Approximately seven miles out into the bay the waters were too shallow for a sea-going tug, even if it had been possible to lift the barge from its resting place and put it back into the water. This recovery presented a number of challenges.

The barge, which looked like a huge department store, was loaded with some four-hundred and fifty tons of cargo destined for Fort Severn. Included were a myriad of items such as snowmobiles and rifles, cans of soup and butter, plus two-hundred tons of oil. This was pumped out, stored in barrels and taken ashore. Anything liquid, of course, froze and thawed as the seasons came and went and the barge sat, apparently abandoned in the wilderness for well over a year.[4]

In the spring of 1974 a decision was made. The remaining supplies would be airlifted them to Winisk and anything salvageable would be sold to the people there. The pilot of one of the DC3's that came to transfer the goods said he would be glad to take any of us out with him to see the barge. Of course I had to take advantage of that offer.

It was strange to be the only passenger in such a large plane flying over the familiar vastness of white, trying to pin point the barge, large as it was, down below. When we finally spotted this speck in the wilderness and landed, we found ourselves in a beehive of activity. Men were running up and down a ramp that had been raised to the entry of the barge, wheeling boxes, cartons and bags down to ground level where they were hoisted into the plane. Skidoos, barrels of gas, clothing, rifles, boxes of shells and food stuffs were all heaped together in one undifferentiated pile and hoisted aboard the plane. There was no organization of goods or plan because none was possible. Although snow lay everywhere, the sun was bright and the frantic activity seemed to warm the participants.

An entry from my journal for March 24/74 reads:

"Right now the big air lift is on from the H.B.C. barge that is marooned out on the Cape. It ran aground last year with thousands of dollars worth of goods on board. The barge itself is worth a quarter of a million. It contains gas and clothing and skidoos and food and canoes and all sorts of things. Apparently some people have been out there and helped themselves to things and now that it is known where the barge is others are thinking of going. So the Bay has organized a big air lift to bring the stuff here and to have it shuttled across to the village where they will sell it. Much of the food is wasted and quite a bit of the goods are either gone or ruined but apparently there is still lots left. The lift begins tomorrow.

Some O.P.P.s came into the village last week to talk to the people about it. But according to Father Daneau they didn't say very much that was helpful. They said that to be accused of stealing you had to have the intent of stealing and if the barge was apparently abandoned for a year and a half they probably thought it was just there for the taking, which wasn't much help."

My jounal entry for April 1, 1974 notes:

"The barge is being unloaded out on the coast and skidoos are racing back and forth like beavers hauling supplies. Everything seems to involve controversy. Ken, the H.B.C. manager fired the clerk Stewart and they came over to ask me to sit in and listen to their argument. I tried to be helpful but

The Hudson's Bay Company barge went aground off Cape Henrietta Maria and was left in the snow for nearly two years. It was finally located and the goods transported by air to Winisk.

probably wasn't. Stewart is now living with Jim and Linda and has to leave on the next sled and Ken is getting a new clerk and the Indians are signing a petition about Treaty Nine have been in complaining about prices in the store and prices for the goods from the barge and the suitability of the food from the barge and the cost of skidoo trips across the river and just about everything else. They were hauling the five miles for five dollars and said they wanted ten. Ken wouldn't give them ten so they refused to haul. Then they changed their minds and said they would haul."

"There are hardly any kids in school as they are all packing boxes for H.B.C. Goods are piled high outside the store and warehouse and everybody is either hauling by skidoo or carrying boxes. It looks like one great ant hill."

Of course with all the freezing and thawing and yanking around, liquids got spilled and all sorts of things intermixed. We

The Oblate Mission, with the telephone receiver disc in the background.

noticed diesel fuel had permeated a lot of the food stuff, particularly boxes of blueberry muffin mix which gave the muffins a peculiar flavour. We ate them anyway, pretending that that was the way they were supposed to taste.

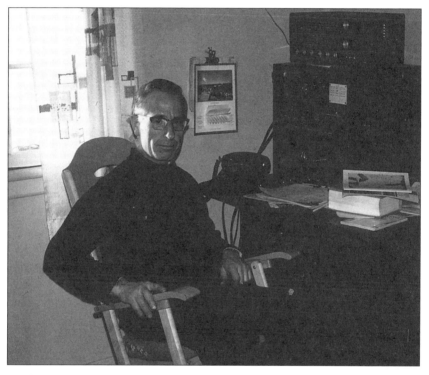

Father Daneau with his radio phone, the only communication to the outside for many years.

YOU ARE YOUR OWN PHYSICIAN

And then disaster struck! I, who had hardly ever been sick a day in my life, woke up one Friday morning with a searing pain in my right eye. George had no idea what was wrong, nor did Father Daneau who kept the medical kit for the village. From it he sent down some eye drops that did no good at all. Father tried to radio out to the Moose Factory hospital for advice and help, but the signals had been out for ten days and no communication was possible. Down the trail a little Native baby lay restless with fever and we could get no help for him either.

All day I walked the floor crying with pain and all night I agonized without sleep. By Sunday the pain had subsided a little, but I had to admit to George that I had almost no sight in my right eye. As I looked around the sitting room all I could see was a square of light from the big front window and shadows everywhere else.

When someone came to ask us to go down and look at the sick baby, both George and I went, despite my eye, and although my knowledge of medicine was nil. The baby was wrapped in blankets and held in the arms of one of the older women who sat in the warmth of the stove. The family lived in the usual little wooden house with a sparsely furnished one long main room and two small bedrooms.

George took the baby's temperature and acknowledged that the fever likely indicated pneumonia. But all we could do was sit with the family or walk the baby up and down, soothing it as best we could. As always the house was filled with people. Most eventually left, but the children who were still there kept waking the baby who he had been placed in its little hammock in a corner. As night fell, the oldest child aged six, lit a candle and set it in the window to light the little room where the baby lay. At the time the father was out in the bush cutting wood as he did each day, dragging it back by hand on a heavy, wooden sleigh since he had neither a snowmobile nor dogs.

The next Saturday, quite unexpectedly, a small plane landed at the base and two tall men arrived in the village by snowmobile.

They were two evangelical missionaries from the Sioux Lookout area where George used to teach. One of them a former pupil, was now an ordained minister. When they saw me they gathered around me with George and offered voluble prayers for my welfare and recovery. The three men, all well over six feet tall formed a kind of teepee over my much smaller frame. They all seemed to stand so close to heaven that I felt sure that God was bound to hear them. They then hurried down the trail to see the sick baby, even though Father Daneau was already there, and offered prayers for it too.

Although the Roman Catholic and Anglican churches were the first to venture into the north following the Hudson's Bay Company and the fur traders, in more recent years Mennonites and Evangelicals established bases in the larger areas from where they sent out missionaries to visit the smaller settlements and hold services. Besides the two men who had landed at Winisk, George had a particular missionary friend called Brian Steed who often called to see George when on his missionary rounds. George had heard that Brian had had a serious accident in the bush, but could not believe the details until Brian arrived one day and told him what had happened.

Besides holding prayer services at the various settlements, Brian was on a commercial run in October, 1968 when he was flying a passenger in a Beaver to an isolated campsite for International Nickel. After he had delivered his passenger, he was scouting a possible supply base for the company on an isolated lake some twenty miles north of Sioux Lookout. He found the spot admirably suited for the Company's purpose. As he was taxiing his plane across the lake for take-off, a gust of wind blew his hat off his head and left it floating in the water. Since the hat was Brian's favourite, he decided to turn the plane around, drop down onto a pontoon and snatch up the hat as it went by.

Brian had warned his previous passenger, and many others, to beware of the spinning propeller and not to get too close to it. He himself was always careful. But he had been hauling oil drums recently and some of the oil had spilled onto both his boots and the pontoons. The slick was such that when a slight pitch caught him, he fell off the pontoon and into the spinning propeller. He felt a whack on his shoulder, then found himself thrashing about in the icy water.

"I didn't know my arm was gone," he told George, "until I tried to swim."

Exerting all the strength he had, Brian managed to hoist himself up onto the pontoon again, crawl up the five-rung ladder and into the cockpit. He had two choices; he could either radio to Sioux Lookout for help and wait until someone reached him, supposing they could find him in the dense bush, or he could try to fly the plane home.

His prayer was "Lord, tell me what to do," and he said the answer came back as clear as his friend's voice, "Fly the plane home."

Of course he would bleed to death if he did not get a tourniquet on his arm to staunch the flow of blood. The best he could do was to wrap his belt around the slippery stump with the other end around his neck and clenched in his teeth. In this way he flew the plane back to Shebandowan Lake from where his friends transferred him to Lakehead General Hospital. There he recovered sufficiently to return to his flying and to his missionary work.

George prepared lunch and diner for the missionaries, after a fashion, while I made up beds for the night. The next day, Sunday, George took them across the river by snowmobile. When he returned he said somewhat sheepishly, "That fellow kissed me when he left." He meant his former tall student. I thought that if he had kissed me it would have made more sense.

On Monday the signals were still out. The pain was not as severe, but the sight was even dimmer. Then the phone rang. It was Father Daneau and the relief in his voice was palpable. Apparently an unexpected plane had arrived, carrying two doctors and a nurse on one of their rare visits to the settlements along the Bay. It did not take them long to diagnose my infection as herpes zoster or shingles, both inside the eye and up through the scalp. There was an urgent need for both me and the sick baby to be transported out for medical treatment.

On these visits the medical people made a quick survey of the village, treating any who come to the mission for help. Towards nightfall, when their visit was over, they took the baby and me across the river to the base where a small Cessna was waiting and loaded us aboard. There were too many people for the size of the aircraft, but no one could be left behind. We all squeezed in and the plane took off.

Immediately following our landing at at Moose Factory the baby was treated and my eye was given a cursory examination and a more professional bandage. Arrangements made for my immediate transfer to the North York General Hospital in Toronto. One of the doctors who had landed at Winisk was from the London University Hospital which periodically sent personnel to the Bay to supplement the treatment by those from Moose Factory. I met him while some Natives and I were waiting for the plane to take off for the south.

"Father Daneau said that if we hadn't arrived he would have brought a plane in for you," the doctor said.

"You can't bring a plane in," I reminded him, "if you can't get a message out, and no messages were possible for the previous ten days and more."

The doctor looked incredulous.

"I don't understand people," he said, "who virtually do without medical attention."

Of course he lived in the heart of London, Ontario where the best medical attention was available constantly. We were people of the North who accepted the conditions that we found there or we didn't venture into the wilderness.

The large patch over my eye afforded me special attention on Air Canada where I was reminded of the neat stewardesses these planes featured, along with newspapers, fresh coffee, snacks and warm interiors. I tried to read the paper with my one good eye, but gave up. My whole body ached with pain and weariness.

At the Toronto airport the commissionaire, who was directing taxis, pushed everyone else aside when I told him I was going to the hospital.

"Take this lady first," he instructed the driver and ushered me into the cab.

At the airport I was reminded that I was in the city, actually the city in which I was born. There was no snow and the people were dressed accordingly, the ladies with high heels, skirts and light jackets. I, on the other hand, was still muffled to my ears in a heavy parka, mitts and snow boots.

"We know who you are," remarked the hospital clerk when I arrived at the desk. "You are from the north and we are expecting you."

That was nice. After preliminary treatment to my eye I snuggled down for my first night in hospital and slept. Eventually I was told that the herpes zoster stemmed from the chicken pox that I had had as a child many years before. The virus had been lying dormant in my system until fatigue or debilitation of some kind allowed it to emerge. While still in the hospital I was called to the telephone one morning and was utterly astounded to hear George's voice.

"Where are you calling from?" I wanted to know because this was not a radio call with the usual static and "Roger—Roger—Do you read me?" and so on.

"I'm calling from Winisk," he replied, explaining that the first Anik A1 satellite that had been sent up the year before now was activated. Phone calls now were possible from Winisk and twenty-five other small settlements of the north to the rest of the country, and indeed to the rest of the world. No longer would we have to rely on the vagaries of the weather and the atmosphere to transmit wireless emergency messages or any other kind of message to the outside world.

From Winisk the voice went up to the satellite from where it bounced down to Allan Park near Hanover in central Ontario and then to Bell's main switching station in Hull, Quebec. From there the voice went anywhere, and all in one third of a second. Replies came back the same way. It was truly something of a miracle and, like the snowmobile, it revolutionized the North. Eventually it would also transmit both radio and television programmes, but at that point we had neither except for rare, partial programmes that once in a while came in on the radio. Sometimes the weather would permit a clear reception from the American south when we were totally unable to reach Toronto.

George tried to tape the first phone call made from Hudson Bay, but since I did most of the talking, all he got was his own voice saying "Yes" and "No."

The Toronto doctor said that he was greatly relieved to hear that now telephone messages were possible. Even after I left hospital the herpes was likely to recur from time to time and I would need additional treatment if I did not want to lose the sight of the eye altogether.

And recurrences did happen. I wasn't back at Winisk very long when I decided to try to get out to get more treatment. The blood vessels were breaking in the eye and sharp pains came and went with alarming regularity. It was all just too much. The river was still floating with ice, but I decided that if I could get across I was going out. George phoned Albert to ask if he would take me.

"Sure, I take your wife," replied Albert. "I leave my wife at home."

We went down to the river bank where a wide ledge of ice jutted out into the river. Albert and George pushed the canoe over the ice into the water and started up the motor. Albert then had to nose through the skin of slush out into the clear channel and tack his way up and down, trying to find a way through to the opposite bank to a place where he could land. We went downstream for quite a distance, then nosed into a shallow spot on the opposite shore and pulled the canoe up onto the ledge of ice that rimmed that bank.

Once up on shore we had to walk about two miles or so, over tundra and through willows and alders that dragged at our clothes like jungle creepers. We continued across frozen ground until we saw the Bombardier sitting on a hill waiting for us. Since they had no idea exactly where we were going to land, the men waited on a height where they could survey as wide a stretch of the shore as possible.

Mike P. from the base, driver of the Bombardier, took us across the open fields, up and down gullies even throwing George on top of me as we hit one of the dips. Finally we reached the air base. There we only had to wait an hour and a half for the plane to take me to Moosonee, on to Timmins and eventually back to Toronto.

In the city, the doctor, sitting in his warm office, cheerfully asked me if I had had a "good trip." I told him I had had a very bad trip, but I don't think he believed me. Sitting in his cosy office, he was unable to picture the half frozen river and the ragged terrain over which I had just travelled. He looked somewhat puzzled at my response, but changed all the medication. Apparently it was the pilocarpine I was taking that was causing the blood vessels to break and the muscles to contract, thus creating the pain I had been experiencing. With the reduced medication I soon felt much better and even could see more clearly.

By the time I got back to Winisk the river was frozen solid and George was waiting for me at the plane with his skidoo. We crossed the river with no difficulty, but, not being able to get up the steep bank on the other side, we had to tack back and forth before we found a place that allowed us to reach the top of the bank and home.

It was wonderful to be back.

AND A FAMILY PHYSICIAN TOO

Under normal circumstances George attended to the medical needs of the village. Father Daneau was the keeper of the medicine chest, but he was happy to turn any medical problems over to George, along with whatever medicines and instruments that were required. George would make the preliminary examination and, if the problem was too serious for local treatment, he would relay his findings to Father. He would pass them on to the hospital at Moose Factory, weather permitting of course.

One day George was called down to see Allan Wabin who was reported sick. He was lying on a bed under a sleeping bag in a tiny house of two or three rooms at the far end of the village. Skins were hanging from the rafters and traps and guns piled in the little porch. One small wood stove heated the house while an Aladdin lamp provided a cheerful light.

As usual when someone was ill, a lot of people crowded into the home. George took Allan's temperature which he reported to Father Daneau who, in turn, sent some penicillin pills down for him. There was a lot of flu in the settlement at the time so that was probably what Allan had. With all the people milling about him there no doubt would be more cases before long.

Sally Koodwat came to our door one day feeling quite ill. I let her sleep on the couch where she stayed for two hours, then I walked her home. Sally had seven children, eight years of age and younger, and they were used to creating bedlam in the three rooms in which they lived. Sally slept with the two youngest children in the main room. Some of the children slept on the floor wrapped in blankets while two others used various beds in the other two rooms.

A few days later I called down to see Sally. She seemed much better since she was out sawing wood with her husband, Douglas. I saw her new baby, not yet a month old, sleeping on a bed in a tikinagan. Another was asleep on a nearby bed, a corner of the comforter in her mouth. The next youngest, wearing little moccasins that Sally had made, sat on a bed playing with some stuffed animals we had given to the family. The four oldest children stood around, wrapped in padded snowsuits swaddled to the eyes.

Bits of meat lay idle in a pan. Sally eagerly gave out the vitamin biscuits I had brought and hefted the bag of powdered milk. I was ashamed that I had not brought more.

George did not have much to do with obstetrics. Nearly all the women in the village, who were expecting babies, went down to Moose Factory two or three weeks before the baby was due and had their babies there. We sometimes thought that they got pregnant just to have a holiday at Moose every year or so.

Jacob Walker's wife was the exception. She had gone once to Moose Factory and determined never to go again. Instead, when she felt the birth imminent, she and her family retreated to a tent in the bush, regardless of the time of year. There the baby was born on a bed of spruce boughs, with only her husband in attendance and her older children close by. The last baby born there, however, had deformities of the legs that might have been prevented if he had been born in a hospital. But who knows? At the last birth, the temperature outside the tent was eight degrees Fahrenheit and not much warmer inside.

One night George was called to see his friend, Albert, who was wheezing and gasping and taking penicillin. George took his temperature, but before he left Albert told him to come back the next day. "And bring some soup," which George did. Both Father and George conferred over Albert that day, trying to decide how much of a dose of penicillin George should give him by injection. Since Albert made a full recovery, they must have judged it reasonably correctly.

Another day Albert came to have George pull out a tooth. His wife, Laura, had tried to wrestle with it using a pair of pliers, but the tooth remained firm. George borrowed Father's forceps and in a moment had Albert's tooth out, much to the satisfaction of both.

Once in a long while a dentist would arrive in the settlement mostly to do extractions. George met both him and Albert at the air base and asked the latter if he had seen the dentist while he was in the settlement. Albert shook his head.

"He no my dentist," he stated, "You my dentist." A statement which gave George some concern but also considerable satisfaction.

One time while we were eating a roast of goose on a Sunday night when Father was there, I bit on a pellet of shot and broke one of my back teeth. George was all for borrowing Father's forceps again and pulling out the damaged molar, but I would have none of it. When I eventually went out to Moosonee where the dentist there did a repair job, George was quite disappointed. He actually put a temporary filling into one of his own teeth which, the dentist he consulted in the south said, couldn't be improved on. George was delighted.

One of the ladies in the village had given premature birth to a pair of twins. They had spent their early weeks in an incubator in Hamilton, Ontario, but were now lying in a bed with their mother, looking so tiny and helpless. George took their temperatures and said that they had a fever, but their colour was good and they were breathing well. One had a swollen scrotum, but it didn't seem to be bothering him. It was the other twin that was crying. A girl was feeding him from a bottle, but it seemed to me that she was letting air into his stomach so perhaps that was the source of the problem. Of course the house was full of people.

George reported his findings to Father who said that nothing could be done that night. We would have to wait until the next day to see how the babies were then. By morning they looked much better and the parents were happier. Father, however, relayed the message to the hospital by radio phone with the doctor replying that we should send the babies out to the hospital until they were stronger. Both left on the next scheduled plane (the Sked) the following Tuesday and stayed in the hospital at Moose Factory for several months.

One night before the twin incident, George got a frantic call from our friend, Alex, to say that Father Daneau had collapsed while saying Mass. George raced down to the church, but Father had recovered and was carrying on as best he could. When George talked to him after Mass, Father said it was just a stomach upset and he was all right. However when the Bishop heard about the incident, he ordered him out for a checkup while Father Gagnon came in to take his place.

Father Gagon was so delighted to be back in his old stamping ground that he hardly could wait to greet the people who were

A Winisk mother with five of her nine boys.

meeting the plane before he jumped on a skidoo and tore down the trail, the first one off the air strip before the plane had even left. He looked as much like the Lone Ranger as a priest could. However, his stay was short as the doctor pronounced Father Daneau fit and well and he was back at Winisk after a few days.

Jacob Walker was the husband of the lady who refused to go to hospital to give birth. One day he came down to ask us to take a look at his wife who, he said, had been beaten up by her brother. They lived in a little one-room house at the end of the village, but he had made an attempt to divide the room in two by means of a partition which was still under construction. Jacob was outside chopping wood when we arrived, but he went in with us and lighted a candle so we could see. His wife was lying on a single bed against one wall while his two older children raced around the room and the third one was leaning up against another wall in a tikinagan. Several more beds stood against the walls and a little tin stove gave out heat. Everything was in unimaginable disarray, with the floor littered with papers and scraps and chips and debris. The table was also covered with odds and ends, including an open lard pail.

The candle gave very little light, but we could see that the woman had a black eye and she showed me the big bruise on her breast where the man either punched or kicked her. She said her head hurt and her arm also. There was little we could do except suggest cold compresses on the bruises and promise to return in the morning to see how she was. George suggested that Jacob go to Father Daneau for aspirin or something similar. The next day when we went back and took her a loaf of bread she seemed much better. The eye was a little more open and she seemed generally brighter.

Just at freezeup Alexandra Gull took ill with what we thought was gall bladder trouble. We couldn't help her very much beyond taking her a loaf of bread and informing Father. He agreed that she should go out to hospital, but getting across the river to the plane was almost impossible with the river partly frozen and partly open. However, a helicopter from an oil drilling rig on Hudson Bay happened to be in the area. It dropped into the village to take Alexandra over to the river to the base to catch the plane to Moose Factory.

The winter before I arrived a woman accidentally was shot in the head with a rifle. Fortunately radio signals were good and a DC3 was called in to take her to hospital. The plane reached the air base all right but fog prevented a landing, requiring it to turn around and return without the patient. The next day the plane came again and air lifted her to Moose Factory. In the meantime she spent the night at the air base, after being pulled across the river in a sleigh behind a skidoo. Despite receiving the very meagre medical attention that Winisk could provide, she did recover reasonably well once under proper care.

One day Rebecca Mack phoned to say that her husband, Jason, had fallen off his skidoo and broken his leg. We went down and there was little doubt that the leg was broken. Jason was sitting on a bed, covered with a multitude of quilts and with a candle for a light. His grandmother, Beula, was putting salve on the leg and attempting to bandage it. All kinds of people were milling around in the house, including Jacob Walker's wife with the baby that had been born in the bush, leaning against the wall in a tikinagan. There was little that George could do about a broken leg, but stabilize it and inform Father that Jason would need to go out to hospital to have the bone set.

Rita Simpson who was eight-four years old, was very sick and lying on a little bed all covered with quilts. She looked small and shrivelled but bright enough with her dark eyes alight. George took her pulse which he said was strong. We came home and cooked some prunes, the last package we had. I took them and some oranges down to her. Two of the other elderly ladies were there, just sitting and waiting. Rita took a few sips of prune juice and kept it down all right, but said she had a severe pain in her abdomen. Father Daneau consulted the doctor by phone and he said he thought she was "sinking fast." However, she was still alive and bright when we left the village a year and a half later.

Through all his years in the north, George had undertaken whatever medical help that the settlements required. He told me one time of a man coming to him with a dislocated shoulder. He put the man down on the floor, put his foot on the man's ribs and yanked his arm until it snapped back into place. He said, with considerable satisfaction, that he could hear the snap when it returned to normal.

Another time at Fort Severn a man cut the top of his foot with an axe. George told one of the children to go down to Grandma Boshey's for a needle and thread which he sterilized and stitched the wound closed.

"He was sitting at the table eating fish," George said with amazement, "and the whole time he didn't miss a bite."

George told him to keep off his feet and to keep the wound dry. The next day he saw the man in the river hauling in his fish nets with the water well over his rubber boots. The wound healed fine.

George had been used to stitching cuts together with needle and thread, but Father Daneau had something in his medical kit called a "butterfly bandage" which pulled the edges of the skin together and held them more neatly until the wound healed. When Stewart Henley had given his foot a cut with an axe similar to the fellow in Fort Severn, the butterfly bandage helped begin the healing, along with penicillin to head off infection.

During one of the hospital's routine medical visits, a young female doctor was in charge, obviously not long out of medical school and very pretty. Since George had been complaining about stomach pains (unrelated to my cooking) I telephoned the doctor to ask her advice.

"Tell him to come down and see me," she suggested, "and I will have a feel of his tummy."

When George came in for lunch I told him that there was a girl at the mission who wanted to have "a feel of his tummy." To my surprise he hurried right down. When he came back I asked him how he got along.

"It was some Grade Seven kid down there," he retorted, "who was trying to tell me what to do, not even Grade Eight." When I later told the doctor what George had said she laughed and admitted that her youthful looks were often a handicap, particularly to older people in which grouping she counted George.

In spite of the lack of medical attention, many of the village people lived to a vigorous old age. Families, and especially grandchildren, watched over the old people, cutting their wood, drawing water for them and making sure that they were warm and well supplied with food. When death occurred everyone helped according to custom.

One cold January day, James Mack's wife, Charlotte, died at age seventy-two. George was with her when she died, along with Father Daneau who gave her the last rites. Just a few days before this George had chopped up a large pile of wood for James and helped him pile it in his house.

I went down later in the day when the women had her laid out on the bed with paper stuffed into her nose and ears. A bag of what looked like salted peanuts was sitting on her chest, probably as sustenance for her journey into the next life. In the basement of our house two women were washing out a blanket, presumably for wrapping around Charlotte in her coffin. Outside, a large bonfire was consuming her clothes and other belongings. James, at age seventy-six, looked quite bewildered. George said he heard him say softly in Cree, "I go too."

For some inexplicable reason one of the men in the village phoned the doctor in Timmins to say that Charlotte might have taken poison. This meant a delay to the funeral in case an autopsy would be required. Father tried all day to reach the coroner, but was unable to do so until very late. The corner said to go ahead and bury Charlotte because he was busy operating in Timmins and could not get away to come to Winisk. The funeral took place the next day in a fierce snow storm. Of course the whole village was in the church to view the coffin covered with a purple cloth, resting at the altar and to pay their last respects. Luke and Xavier, two of James Mack's grandsons, stood solemnly on each side of Father Daneau. I could not help but admire their beautiful, dark faces.

Alexandra led the chanting, but broke down part way through and the congregation had to continue without her. James sat at the back, impassive and quiet. At the end of the service they removed the purple cover and the lid of the box underneath so James could see his wife one more time. One of his granddaughters took pictures, standing on a seat and using her Instamatic camera. A man hammered the lid on the coffin, nail after nail while Father continued to read the service. In spite of the cold, the men had dug a deep grave in the cemetery at the end of the village where everyone congregated through the blowing snow. The service completed, the men shovelled earth on top of the coffin and the people went away.

Some group in Toronto called the "Canadian Progress Group" had sent some mattresses to the village and George took one down to James' house because much of their belongings had been destroyed, as was the custom after a death. Although it was just a foam pad covered with a cotton cover, the ladies in the house were so glad to get it. A few days later one of the women said that James wanted to see George and me. When we called into his house he presented me with a lovely pair of moosehide mitts and moccasins, all beaded and beautiful.

"Kaa nondwiinzeen shonias," he insisted, meaning that he did not want any money for them. Of course I burst into tears.

NO ONE WENT WITHOUT

Food was a constant concern, not because we did not have enough, but because choice was almost non-existent. An outfitter in Timmins would send in food by mail which was the cheapest way at 66 cents a pound, or sometimes we could get a box of goodies slid aboard a charter out of Moosonee for nothing. The Winisk store had basic supplies of canned goods and occasionally some perishables, but they were very expensive and strictly limited.

In the fall of 1973 the two-month mail strike hit the country and cut off our food shipment altogether. No one went hungry as the people of the village made sure that whatever food they had was shared equally among all residents. We would pay for the chunks of caribou they bought us, but eventually even that ran out and we were reduced to a diet of porridge and goose. Every morning we had porridge with reconstituted milk. At noon we had roasted goose, unadorned; dinner at night consisted of cold goose. We did have the bread I baked and instant coffee, a diet that grew increasingly monotonous.

When the people brought us a goose it was already plucked and cleaned with the opening stitched together with a goose feather. They never charged us (nor the other 'old people') for these birds and we were grateful for as long as there was any food at all in the village, everyone shared. Once we were delighted when our neighbour brought us some beaver meat, truly a delicious treat.

One day a Bell Telephone man arrived with fresh food from the 'outside,' most of which he left with us. There were actually tomatoes and green onions, and oranges and candies. It was the tomatoes that overwhelmed us. Before going to bed that night we gorged on two big, fat, juicy tomato sandwiches, finishing off the last four slices of a loaf of bread from the store. The store had no more bread, nor even bread mixes which it usually carried. Again I had to make bread from scratch using outdated yeast. I had no mixing bowls, but mixed the dough in a roasting pan and set it to rise on the lid over the hot air register. The result was edible, but that is about all you could say for it.

Since ours was the only oven in the village, one of Alex's sons used to come to bake bread for his family. Robert was about ten years old and was almost never seen without his crocheted hat with the tassels dangling. However, he did a wonderful job of sifting and kneading and setting the dough to rise. The dough, of course, was in much better condition when there was no mail strike and the yeast reasonably fresh, but regardless, the smell of the bread coming out of the oven was delectable. His brother, Luke, took a fancy to pies which could be bought as mixes in the store with canned fruit for filling. Since George rather fancied himself as a pie maker he was the one to oversee Luke's efforts and I think they turned out quite well.

I often wondered why the store stocked mixes since there was only one oven in the entire village. Along with bread and pie mix, the store also sold cake mixes which the people would bring to me from time to time to bake for them. One was a wedding cake for which I followed the directions as best I could. However I did not know that the cake should remain in its pan till it cooled before being turned out and cut. As a result the cake fell apart in my hands and the party had wedding pudding instead of cake. Still, nobody complained, at least not in my hearing.

For another wedding the bride said she wanted three layers which I did my best to provide. But the top cake cracked and slid off the other two even though I tried to anchor it with knitting needles which did not help very much. I finally scrapped the top layer and made another one which I froze to see if that would give it any stability, patching up cracks and other imperfections with icing. Two girls took it away in a skidoo and I just hoped it was satisfactory.

This wedding took place late in the afternoon. The bride, groom, best man and bridesmaid sat at the front of the church until after Father had said Mass. They then stood for the wedding ceremony while half a dozen boys swarmed over the altar taking pictures. Since the principles never turned to face the congregation it was the only way they could snap their faces. Afterwards everyone went outside to wait for them although it was pitch dark by that time. More people tried taking pictures while others threw rice. Soon the bridal couple were lost in the darkness so everyone went home. A party later that evening would be held in the Community Hall where my pitiful cake would be featured as part of the supper. I was glad I wouldn't be there to see it.

Since Albert's wife was up country hunting with a couple of other ladies, Albert came in for something to eat at our place. I gave him and the boys the remains of the broken cake which they ate eagerly, even though George said that it tasted of fuel oil.

The next day Albert's skidoo broke down while he was out hunting, but George met him and brought him back home. I asked Albert if he wanted coffee when he came in. "Yes," he said, "and cookies too." I did my best to oblige.

As mentioned, food was expensive at Winisk. When shipping costs were added we could expect prices as follows:

	Toronto	Moose	Freight	Winisk
Potatoes–10 lb.	$.34	$1.04	$3.20-$4.60	$5.50
Bread–1 1/2 lb	$.50	$ .48	$ .48-$ .69	$1.30
Eggs–1 doz-2 lb.	$.66	$ .95	$ .64-$ .92	$2.00
Butter–1 lb.	$.91	$1.05	$ .32-$.46	$1.39
Oranges –1 doz.	$.50	$ .79	$1.28-$1.84	$3.16

Once during the mail strike we placed an order for food totalling $108 from the Hudson's Bay store at Moosonee, then paid $107 to ship it in. Included were a crate of apples and a crate of oranges, most of which George gave away to the children and to any who were sick in the village. We also ordered three crates of eggs and quite a number of them George gave away as well. If we were expecting fresh food when the plane came in we had to be at the base to meet it, otherwise all would all freeze before we got it home.

The air strike caused more problems than the shipment of food. Some time in the fall the Winisk parents mailed out their orders for Christmas gifts for their children, but due to the strike none of the orders reached the store. What would they do for Christmas?

As the holiday drew near a lady from next door came in ask my advice and she burst into tears.

"We have nothing for the children," she said, "and we don't know what to do."

I don't think that I had ever seen a Native person cry before no matter how tough the times became. I didn't know what to tell her.

The strike ended just before Christmas, but there was no time then to place new orders. In a hurry the chief and council phoned to the fire brigade in Timmins that had sent toys to the Winisk children before. An emergency effort was launched and just before Christmas a load of gifts arrived. The village was very grateful, especially the parents.

Once in a while the Hudson's Bay Company manager and his wife would invite us to dinner. On these rare occasions, they would serve all the good things that we couldn't get—such as fresh milk, mushrooms, ice cream and steak, We were never sure if they realized what a banquet these items made for us.

From time to time George's brother, Carman, was a tremendous help in sending food in to us. One shipment contained perking coffee, prunes, detergent for the dishes, bran muffin mix, bread mix and a lot of other lovely things. If there were fresh foods such as apples, we shared them with the children who accepted what we offered graciously, and left us in appropriate time to enjoy what was left by ourselves.

As noted before we usually had lots of geese or caribou and sometimes a duck or two that George might happen to shoot. Occasionally the people would bring in a boatload of fish. The catch would be bountiful and they would just tell us to go down to their boat and help ourselves to whatever we needed. One time Alex's family caught a pike, weighing twelve pounds and measuring forty inches, which they very generously gave to us. George undertook to cook a fish one night in what he thought was an exotic batter made from butter and three precious eggs, and flavoured with celery salt. It was terrible and ruined the fish.

With ours being the only home freezer in the village, usually it was filled with other people's food. Most geese that were shot in the fall were smoked in the smoke tents, but more were deposited in our freezer, feathers and all. Even the store kept meat in the

The oil stove in the school doubled as a cookstove for preparing a warm breakfast.

freezer. Usually it was so full of other people's food that there was little room for our own, whenever we had any extra to freeze.

At Hallowe'en the store brought in bags of candy, but the cost was $1.05 a bag, twice the price one would pay outside. As an alternative I made popcorn balls with some left over popcorn, some molasses and some rather crummy sugar flake cereal. Altogether I made up fifty little bags. So many people came Hallowe'en night, dressed in all kinds of clothes and makeup that I had to make more. The children loved it.

Very kind groups in the south used to send in boxes of clothing and, although George always had the children write letters of thanks, I doubt that they ever really knew how much the clothing meant. When the boxes arrived the house would be full of people trying on clothing and shoes, sorting baby clothes and going home with all sorts of things they really needed but otherwise could not obtain. Some bundles contained comic books which the children snatched up then stretched out on the floor, reading and looking at the pictures. George always took out items that he thought would suit the old people who never came, but were grateful for the things he took to their houses. If the clothes did not fit, they passed them on to someone that they did fit.

Little Alex Johns came in one day with no mitts and no parka but only a heavy shirt in November weather with the temperature at 15 degrees Fahrenheit. The shirt was lacking a top button, leaving his neck and chest all bare. Although I sewed a button on it did not help much. The year before we had brought in a new parka especially for him, but he took it home and came back without it. We never saw it again.

Mail, of course, was terribly important, coming in only twice a month and sometimes not even that. Sometimes the postmaster in Moosonee forgot to put the mail on the plane and sometimes the manager in the Winisk store was so slow in sorting that we would not get it until the following day, all very maddening. One mail day little Danion Hunter and Ivan pulled up chairs on each side of me and peered intently at all the letters I opened, although neither of them could read a word. I gave them some prunes which they ate, spitting the pits out on the carpet. However the carpet had seen much worse than that.

A helicopter landed in front of the store, staying close at hand at breakup in case of a flood.

Supplies and personnel arrive by plane as no roads link these settlements with the south.

Food was not the only thing affected by erratic mail deliveries. On October 30, I received a registered letter that had reached Moosonee on September 28. It was a notice from the income tax department stating it was taking legal action if my income tax was not paid within fifteen days, which was fifteen days before I had received the notice. Credit card companies were threatening to cut off our service if we didn't pay our bills, but the bills didn't reach us so we could pay them. The people of the village couldn't get their welfare cheques and the whole problem was impossible to explain to agencies in the south. All we could do was throw up our hands and pay whatever bills we eventually received.

Now and then Jacob Walker would come in all covered with frost, having come from his camp in the bush. We would give him bacon and eggs if we had them and a bundle of clothes for his wife and children, also if we had them. When his wife had the new baby, he said he had neither diapers nor baby food. I tore up some sheets to use for the baby and gave him a tin of powdered milk. I also happened to have some Johnson's baby powder which I didn't like to lose, but figured that the baby's needs were greater than mine and therefore parted with it.

On our first Christmas at Winisk we had a party for the children although we had little to give them. I made bags of candy with what I had and bought more at the store till it was all gone. Some of the people brought us gifts of moccasins, a beaded doll and other things they had made.

For my part I tried to crochet little hats for most of the children in the school. I rarely had wool as such, but often had to unravel knitted items that I didn't need in order to make the hats. I have a picture in my mind of little Danion, sitting on the arm of my chair with his arm across the back, waiting for me to finish his hat which he proudly wore home. At one point I had managed to bring in a bundle of baby wool. My intention was to crochet a hat and booties for each baby that was born, but so many babies arrived it was difficult to keep up with the demand.

Unexpectedly a Catholic Sister, who was part Cree herself and spoke the language fluently, came in from Fort Albany. She came down to the house to visit us and told us that the people were pleased with us, but were too shy to tell us.

"They feel their children are loved," she said. Of course they were. How could it be otherwise?

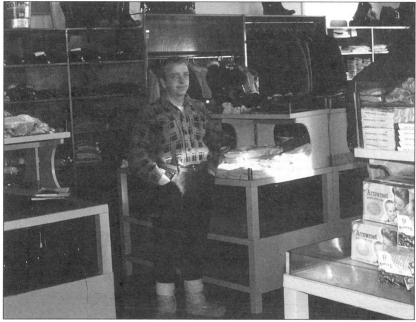

The Hudson's Bay Company store manager poses with his goods.

WHEN TENSIONS RISE

————— ◼ —————

But life was not always serene in the village. Because Winisk was so remote it was usually difficult to obtain liquor. But once in a while a few of the men managed it, and then problems could arise. George, who had been raised in an Evangelical household, had been a non drinker all his life. This he felt was of particular importance if one was living on a reserve.

"Of course you could always make home brew," he remarked one day when we were discussing the question. I thought for a few minutes, then took his hand and led him down to one of the back bedrooms. From under the bed I pulled out a crock filled with my version of home brew—yeast, raisins, sugar and dear knows what all else. If I could experiment with bannock, I could surely experiment with home brew.

George took one startled look at the concoction then collapsed on the floor in laughter, kicking his long legs in the air. But I had no more luck with the home brew than with the bannock. It too had to be thrown out. The dogs, already sceptical about my cooking, regarded the mixture with scorn.

Trouble was rare and usually attributed to no more than two or three people who caused concern to the entire village. Since police were far away in Moosonee, someone would come running for George when a problem arose. "George, you come fix Peter Wheiste. He got a gun. He shoot everybody."

Peter Wheiste lived by himself at the far end of the village. Now and then he was known to buy a large quantity of raisins with which he made home brew. With no apparent concern for his own safety, George went off to the end of the village, opened the door of Peter's house and took away his gun. Peter was standing in the midst of the disarray of his kitchen, a mound of mash in a corner and debris strewn everywhere. Being so tall, George was able to reach over Peter's shoulder and remove the rifle, empty it of shells and put it high up on a shelf with the shells somewhere else. George began to clean up the house, shovelling the mound of mash out the door and putting a pot of coffee on the stove.

"Now, Peter," he admonished, "You are upsetting your mother acting like this and you don't want to upset her do you?"

Peter just stood in the middle of the room and made no reply. George continued bustling about the house, sweeping the floor and disposing of litter either in the stove our out the door. He continued to natter on about Peter not upsetting his mother who lived close by. Eventually after making Peter sit down and drink a considerable amount of coffee, George returned home, still talking about Peter's mother.

When we were out in the summer, the O.P.P. had been called into the village on the same errand when Peter once again was threatening all and sundry with his rifle. The police told George that they approached Peter's house cautiously by way of the drainage ditch, watching the window closely to see whether Peter was going to break it in preparation for firing at them.

"If that window broke," they said, "we were ready to hit the ditch." George seemed to have no such qualms.

Breaking people's windows was a common form of retaliation, serious retribution in Hudson Bay weather in January when the weather had been between 30 and 40 degrees below zero Fahrenheit. Once when a particularly fierce wind blowing was blowing, we found sixty-nine year old Henrietta James and her son living in a tent at the end of the village. Someone had broken the windows in their house and wrecked their home. The tent, about eight by ten feet, had a wooden frame part way up the walls and a canvas roof on top. Two single beds took up most of the space, but melting snow was coming in on one of them. A tin stove with a stove pipe thrust through the top provided heat. Some geese were hanging over the stove and pieces of fish were impaled on a stick leaning against the wall.

I sat on the dry bed while George sat on the floor from where we talked and laughed and had a good visit. Outside, dogs and a collection of gear were scattered along the ground near a nice, clean teepee for smoking meat. There, strung by their necks, were geese hanging on a pole.

One day Michael came into the house in tears. He said that some woman at the other end of the village had taken exception to something he had said or done. She had broken all the windows in his house. Fortunately George knew where there was a stack of glass in the store room at the air base, so he and Michael went over to get sufficient glass to replace them, and Michael was happy again.

Even Father Daneau had his front window broken at one time because he sent a lady's daughter out to hospital for treatment, but not her son. The doctors at Moose Factory finally agreed to take the son who had had a history of mental problems. Once again George went over to the base for a new glass and helped Father install it.

One night in mid-winter when George was out somewhere, an Indian Affairs employee named John came in and tried to have a meeting in our house with the chief and one of the counsellors. But Sam Edwards, who had been out to Moose Factory for a while, came in quite drunk. He ranted and raved at the men until some gave up and went home. Sam had a bottle in his pocket and had been drinking all afternoon. At times he was hysterical, threatening to hit John who was as white as a sheet. Sam kept shouting, "You made them sign, Johnny!", apparently under the impression that this was an original treaty signing. I finally made a pot of coffee which I tried to get Sam to drink but without success. When George came home he calmed Sam down and sent him on his way.

John had come in on a charter bringing a load of welcome groceries for us. I took him back across the river by snowmobile to retrieve the groceries from his plane before they froze. I was nervous about making the trip by myself with only my passenger for direction, but George was in school and couldn't go. However, knowing that the Bay Company manager was somewhere on the trail with some other men, I managed all right except for freezing a strip of skin around my wrist where the skin was bare. When one is all alone on a frozen river with nothing but empty whiteness from horizon to horizon, one's frailty is too abundantly clear.

That night our neighbour Robert came in to see if he could go to Moosonee. He had heard that there was word of his youngest brother who had mysteriously disappeared the previous October. George went in to see Robert the next morning to caution him to go to the police if he suspected somebody who might be responsible and not to accost the man himself. Since Robert was a big man with a quick temper, George was worried. It was not until after breakup that Robert's brother was found at Moosonee, his body frozen under the ice.

When the new Hudson's Bay Company manager, named Tom, arrived at Winisk, George warned him never to offer liquor to any of the men of the village. Although there were only a very few who suffered from alcoholism, those few could cause a great deal of trouble, out of all proportion to their numbers. For whatever reason Tom discounted George's advice. One night he served beer to the men who were playing pool with him in the store. Of course, one of the men, Isaac got too much to drink and broke up the party. Later that night he went back to the manager's house and demanded more beer. Isaac was a big man and Tom was small and thin. To pacify him Tom gave him another bottle or two. However Tom's wife had had enough of this performance. She marched out and sent Isaac packing.

About two o'clock that same morning Isaac came knocking at our door. Although the weather was bitterly cold, he was wearing only a short jacket and low shoes and could have frozen to death. For about an hour there was a long discussion in our kitchen, about I don't know what, with George trying to get Isaac to drink large mugs of coffee. The only conversation I could hear was Isaac's frequent comment, "George, you're preposterous."

At last Isaac set off home into the frigid night. To make sure he got there safely George waited briefly, then phoned his house, then Isaac himself answered. He must have gone like lightening to have reached home so quickly.

The year before I came to Winisk, George told me about the young man who at that time lived in his house and gave lessons to the adults in the classroom in the evening. For some reason some men thought that this fellow was being too friendly with the girls of the village. They surrounded the house one night demanding that he come out so they could beat him up. He, of course, was smart enough not to go even near the door. The men then laid newspapers around the foundation of the house and set them on fire. That was enough for George who yanked open the door, stamped the fire out with his size fourteen feet, and dispersed the crowd who never came back. From then on the tutor held his classes in the basement of the house so he would no longer have to walk back and forth through the village at night.

It was Albert who told me about an incident at Fort Severn where George had taught, about one-hundred miles farther west along the Hudson Bay coast. There George lived in a disreputable shack attached to the school, where the wind blew through the cracks and the roof threatened to part company with the walls. For insulation George improvised with rolls of toilet paper which he stuffed into the cracks and the line of separation between the walls and the roof. None of it seemed to help a great deal. It was here that George one day received a whole carton of furniture polish from Indian Affairs. He had no furniture whatsoever which he could improve by polishing nor would he dream of applying any if he had.

One Christmas George stayed at Fort Severn rather than go out to his home in Southern Ontario. On New Year's Eve the Hudson's Bay Company clerk, supported by a group of young people of the settlement, knocked at George's door and asked if they could hold a dance in the tiny classroom. George knew such an affair would go on all night with raucous music and possibly liquor in evidence. When he refused permission to use the school, the clerk became extremely abusive, swearing and calling George inappropriate names. The story Albert told me was that in the midst of this tirade, George picked the fellow up, swung him over his head and threw him through the air.

"He landed on his feet," laughed Albert, "and he just kept right on running." Albert slapped his knee as he roared with laughter.

I asked George if the story were true, but he just smiled.

"When I looked out the door a few minutes later," he admitted, "there was not a soul in sight. It was as if they had all just melted into the bush."

One night a plane flew in from Severn. A few minutes later we received a phone call from the base that the Severn teacher was there, along with two Native people. This teacher was anxious to meet George. I tidied up the house in preparation for meeting him, not knowing if he would be staying all night. When he arrived he was a flimsy bit of a thing, all hair and whiskers, with turned-in moccasins and patched jeans. In his pocket was a half bottle of whisky; the other half was in the teacher. He was so cold and so befuddled that I had to unbutton his coat for him and sit him down to get warm.

According to him, he was an American draft dodger, divorced from his first wife and two children. He was now married to his second wife who was teaching with him at Fort Severn. He said that he had heard so many stories about George that he thought he must be just like Grey Owl and he had to meet him. He kept repeating this sentiment over and over again. I made up a bed for him, but he said he could walk back to the base and several times attempted to start out on the trail. He would never have made it. George eventually drove him back by skidoo, with the gentle admonition to take care of himself.

When George came back from the base I started to say something to him, "George—" I began, but he interrupted.

"Don't call me George," he remarked, "Just call me Grey Owl," and he laughed heartily.

Charlie and Jessie Matthews, who had come with the teacher from Severn, came in later to have coffee and sandwiches. We had a nice visit, exchanging news of both settlements. They said they had no coffee at Severn so I gave them our bottle of instant brew. Off they went to visit other friends in the village. We did not see any of them again although we heard the plane departing the next morning about 8:30 a.m.

Now that the phone was operating, the people of Fort Severn sometimes called George. An Archie Stoney phoned one night to say that they still talked about him there and wanted him to come back. Later in the fall Archie phoned to say that a DC3 had crashed that week end just off the Fort Severn runway. The pilot and his four passengers, construction men from Winnipeg who were building the new Fort Severn school and going home for a weekend break, were all killed. The cause of the crash was never determined.

When the time came for the re-election of a chief, representatives arrived in from Indian Affairs at Moose Factory. They attempted to hold a nomination meeting in the hall, but all did not go well. People were nominating each other indiscriminately, while one fellow seconded every motion that was made. At that point Sam Edwards came in with a bottle in his back pocket and demanded that proceedings start all over again so he could record them for Treaty Nine.

Some fellow called George Quapit, in from Moose Factory, was also running for Chief although no one was quite sure whether he was even a band member. His name could not be found on the band list anyway. Shortly afterwards he appeared at our door with a little bag of toiletries saying that he wanted a bath. People came for lots of things, but that was the first time anyone had come for a bath. We were so surprised that we let him have one.

The meeting was anything but a success. The party from Moose Factory stayed over night then hoped to leave the next day, on the hospital charter that was coming to take out the medical team working in the village at the time. When a plane did land at the base, and the Bombardier came over the river, everyone thought it was the hospital charter, and a grand exodus followed. At the base they discovered that it was a fuel plane and that the charter would not arrive until much later. Everybody therefore came back to the village, running in and out of our house and making phone calls to the base, to Moose Factory and up and down the village. Jonas Adams suggested that the Indian Affairs Branch men stay in the village until the following week when the regular plane would come in. Such an idea was not well received by those involved. They did not relish spending the better part of a week lounging about in Winisk with nothing to do, when they could have been revelling in the bright lights of Moose Factory. Finally the hospital plane came and everyone left, allowing peace to descend on the village once more.

Some time later another party came in and the meeting for the election of Chief went off much more smoothly. This time the ballot box was carried from house to house. When the ballots were counted, young Gerald Thomas was the newly elected leader.

The major question he and the councillors had to deal with was the future of the store. The Hudson's Bay Company was phasing out all its outpost stores, including the one at Winisk, because they were no longer profitable. Since the village needed the store, the Band wanted the government to help them take the store over by subsidizing it by one hundred thousand dollars a year, the

Smoke tents along the Winisk River.

amount representing the annual loss. After much negotiation they did manage the store, operating as it efficiently as the Bay had done, but with government help.

In spite of the prevalence of candles, wood stoves and coal oil lamps, we had very few fires in the village. One day, however, just at supper time, Alex's smoke tent went up in flames. Everybody came running, fearing it might be a house. Alex's wife, Rose, was in the middle of everything, throwing geese out of the flames while the boys ran back and forth with pails of water. All helped except little Ivan who stood back by himself, sobbing his heart out. Rose, in her distress, was shouting at the boys at a great rate and aiming blows at them with a stick while they dodged out of her way as they tried to douse the flames. Along with the others, George and I helped carry things out of the tent and take down the boards that formed part of the frame.

Next to the smoke tent was a fire on which they were boiling pots of geese for canning, although I am not sure just how this was

112

Smoke tent used for preserving fresh game and fish such as Arctic char.

done. Everybody was going around eating pieces of charred meat, including us, although it was hard to tell whether we were eating burnt goose or charred fish. As soon as the fire was out, our house as usual was full of people who came to try on clothes that the Salvation Army had sent from the south. One little girl with a torn coat and little, worn shoes looked to be in special need. George found her both coat and shoes that were a great deal better than the ones she was wearing.

Alex's boy, Abraham, brought over a big box of leftover meat for the eagle which was still in the basement at that time. George cut the meat up for freezing although nearly all our freezer units were full. Father had commented one time that the eagle, like so many others, was on welfare since all his food and shelter needs were provided for without any effort on his part.

Life in Winisk had its share of ups and downs. Fortunately "troubles" were usually settled with limited fuss and peace would reign once more in this northern village.

LIFE AS A NORTHERNER

—————— ■ ——————

Like so many other northerners, we found that our greatest problem was not with the environment but with bureaucracy.
Northern questions cannot be solved by regulations formulated to
deal with southern situations. Generally each situation in the
north is unique. Our local superintendent in Moose Factory had
never lived in the north. His previous position, as a teacher in the
London, Ontario area, did not equip him to deal with this new
environment. Unfortunately he could not cope with any new situation without first consulting the regulations, which usually had
no relevance to the problem at hand.

One time during the long mail strike, I heard that the
Department of Indian Affairs was sending a charter to Winisk
which would be coming in empty and taking out a passenger. It
seemed sensible to take advantage of this opportunity. In great
excitement I phoned the Hudson's Bay Company at Moosonee for
an order to be placed on the plane—fresh vegetables, fruit, milk,
bread, eggs, salt and all the other items we had not seen for weeks.
On checking with the Indian Affairs Branch office the day of the
flight, I was told by the administrator that the plane was leaving
from Timmins and would not stop at Moose Factory. My order
could not be delivered. I asked if he could not request the plane to
stop at Moose, but he refused because it might cost a little extra
money. In great disappointment I phoned the Hudson's Bay
Company and cancelled. The store manager was not a bit pleased
because it had taken a clerk considerable time to put the order
together, and now it all had to be all taken apart again.

When the plane did arrive at the base the pilot said that he had
stopped at Moose anyway and easily could have brought in the
order. As it was, he brought the plane in totally empty. I could
have cried. About a week later, an Indian clerk in the Moose office
phoned to say that another charter was coming into Winisk and
did I want to put an order on it.

"But will it stop at Moose?" I wanted to know.

"I'll make darned good and sure it does stop," the clerk

declared, "Just tell me what you want and I'll see that it is on board." And he did. When the goods arrived we sank our teeth into tomatoes and oranges and celery and all the things we had been missing. I will always remember that fellow though I don't know his name. I just know he was a true northerner.

One day Sarah from next door came in. She asked us to phone Moose Factory to see if her three boys could go to the Albany residential school because Robert, her husband, was away. She needed to go out for an operation. I phoned the superintendent who said he would let her know. A day or two later he sent in word that the boys could not go to Albany because it was not "in accordance with regulations." He also added that sending the boys to Albany would "allow parents to evade their parental responsibilities." Looking pale and shaken, Sarah said she would see if she could find someone in the village to look after the children. She was not very hopeful, however, as most families were out on the trapline and for those staying in the village, it was all they could do to look after themselves. Apparently the superintendent didn't care, or he maybe didn't know.

On our first trip together into Winisk the superintendent insisted that George attend an 'Orientation' course along with the new teachers, even though it meant that we would miss the regular scheduled plane and would need a charter to reach Winisk when the orientation was over. Since George had spent nearly twenty years in the north and the previous two years at Winisk, this orientation seemed a bit superfluous, but he went to the meeting as required.

He said that the morning was spent learning how to get a travel advance with which to pay for motel and transportation. I met the new Regional Director that day who said it was all nonsense. Motel and airline companies would just submit the bills to his office as they always did and he would pay them. At first it has been first demanded that the teachers pay these items out of their own pockets and he would reimburse them some time later. This nearly precipitated a riot since very few teachers had any money at all the first of September.

Whenever teachers went into the north they always tried to take as much fresh food as possible with them on the plane. Fresh food was almost non-existent in remote locations and shipping costs prohibitive. We were told that we didn't need to take anything since the Winisk store was adequately stocked. In actual fact the store shelves were almost empty at this point. However, in spite of many delays and interference we managed to gather our food together, only to be informed that there would be no charter. We would have to spend a week in Moose Factory waiting for the next scheduled plane. Moose Factory was no place to spend a week twiddling our thumbs while our fresh food rapidly deteriorated. Anyway we should have been in Winisk starting our work which was where we wanted to be.

I blew my top at this point. The chartered plane materialized. On board the same flight were also numerous bags of cement for building a new water cistern at Winisk. When these bags finally arrived in Winisk, they were found to be as hard as a rock and good for nothing as far as I could see.

There was still a considerable amount of baggage that had not arrived with me when I first came to Winisk. I had expected that the Indian Affairs Branch would pay for its transport as they did with all their personnel when they moved from one place to another. The administrator refused, reasoning that when George had first joined Indian Affairs he was single. There was nothing in the regulations allowing him to acquire a wife and belongings somewhere along the way. The cost of shipping these goods was considerable and more than I could afford. Not to be stymied, I appealed to my former boss in Toronto who in turn called Moose Factory. In short order all was delivered.

In return for reasonable consideration by those in authority, we in the field were always happy to spend any amount of extra time and effort on any project that would be helpful to the people, regardless of either precedence or regulations. But things generally went along in a more or less steady course, with George going to school each day and me trying to maintain some semblance of normality in the house. Like most northerners, I was soon quite adept at circumventing both bureaucracy and so-called 'regulations.'

Shortly after I arrived, I thought it would be a good idea to establish a preschool class in the community hall, although the venue was anything but suitable. Since preschool classes were fortunately in

One of the Mission buildings that housed the school and the church.

accordance with regulations, the Moose Factory office agreed (though reluctantly) to purchase suitable toys and other equipment. Two young women would go around the village each morning with a skidoo and sleigh to pick up the preschoolers whose parents wanted them to attend. They would also drop them back at their doors after classes. This would free their mothers to go out into the bush to cut wood or do whatever other chores were required.

The hall was about fifty feet long and half that width, with a long barrel stove in the middle. Chunks of wood were piled underneath it to dry. An iron railing ran around the stove to try to keep the children away from it. There was little heat, however, as the floor was of plywood and very cold. Along the walls were benches used when movies were shown there, as well as the odd table and broken chair left over from some earlier frolic. At the far end were several offices piled with junk, all in complete disorder. They were closed off from the main room by a door and by a glass window over which was draped the screen for the movies on one side and a maple leaf flag on the other.

117

George Hubbert with students.

Two students in a Winisk classroom.

The children were all bundled up in skidoo suits, mitts, hoods and boots. Each child with a flanelette cloth tied around his neck, presumably with which to wipe his nose. In the hall the children took off their jackets but little else. With the enthusiasm of the two girls in charge providing energy and direction, the classes continued through most of the winter. Despite their best efforts, it was unlikely they achieved any remarkable breakthrough in early childhood education, but there were some positives. Although a few of the mothers refused to send their children because they did not agree with the choice of the two teachers, most families responded. A number were happy to have time to deal with other chores and the children enjoyed the books and dolls, and other toys that the classes offered.

On most weekends the men would go hunting and often George went with them. Sometimes he brought home a duck or a goose although I was never sure whether he had shot the bird himself or one of the other men had done so. Tactfully, I never enquired, but just plucked and cooked the bird.

Just before the first big storm in January, Tom from the Hudson's Bay Company and some of the younger men went out to hunt caribou, but they had to hole up in the bush until the blizzard passed. This one was particularly fierce, forcing most people to remain in their houses all day. Our neighbour, Robert, however, came in to our place even before I was dressed. Shortly thereafter the boys, then Michael, then Alice and Patrick arrived. They were followed by Lister, who asked if he could wash some clothes in the basement. His family had a particularly difficult time, both because of a mentally disabled girl who was incontinent and because of the recent arrival of tiny twin babies. Washing clothes was a daunting task in their household. While the store did stock disposable diapers, people could use them only when they could afford the cost. Before long, Sally and her two little ones came in and the house was full.

Gradually the people would begin to disperse and, by night time, we were again alone, although everyone's thoughts were on the men snowbound in the bush. Several days went by at 25 degrees below zero Fahrenheit, when, just as night was falling, Tom's wife, Kitty, saw their lights coming over the river from the

Michael Hunter Sr. displays a caribou recently shot.

Robert Hunter carries on the hunting tradtion.

A young hunter with skins ready to be stretched.

121

direction of the air base. Everyone rejoiced to see them back even though they had seen no caribou and Albert had frozen his cheek.

One fall George went hunting with Tom, hoping to shoot a caribou. For the night they camped on the bank of a river, a short distance up from the water's edge. George wandered down the bank where the ground was soft and marshy. Taking up a small stone, he bent down and made a number of marks in the mud, imitating the foot prints of a caribou as much as he could. He then went up to the tent and asked Tom if he would go down for some water. Tom did so, but almost immediately came tearing back, yelling that there was a caribou down there because he saw the fresh tracks in the mud. Tom was so excited that he rushed in, grabbed his rifle, then tried to rush out with the rifle held sideways. Of course, the gun hit the sides of the tent bouncing Tom right back into the tent landing on his back. He recovered very quickly, but could not understand why George was rolling around on the ground outside, helpless with laughter.

"I knew it wasn't a caribou," he muttered when he finally grasped the situation.

Since hunting was the staple industry of the village, every house had caribou skins hanging to dry, along with muskrat pelts in various stages, and otter skins stretched on wooden, sleeve-like boards, and beaver pelts laced to willow frames.

Winisk was really part of the Polar Bear Park with bears on the distant periphery of the village much of the time. Only Native people were allowed to shoot the polar bears on a quota basis—so many bears per settlement per year. When Antoine shot one, we went down to see it. This magnificent animal was on its back lashed to the sleigh which Antoine had used to haul it from the tundra. It would have weighed somewhere between four hundred and five hundred pounds. George stretched out alongside it, but the bear was longer than he was. Since George was six foot four, the bear must have been close to seven feet as its length was well beyond his.

When Xavier Patrick shot a bear, he gave us some of the meat. George fried it in the pan, but the animal was so beautiful that I hated to eat it. We knew of course, that the liver was deadly poison and could not even be given to the dogs.

Late one night, David Kakakaspan came banging at our door. When George opened it, David cried in great excitement, "Where's your gun? Get me your gun!" Before he would do that, George wanted to know what David wanted to shoot.

"There is a polar bear on the ice," he cried. "Right in front of your house."

I peered out the front window, but could only see the great expanse of white snow and ice that stretched from the river bank right to the horizon. George's gun happened to by lying on the rug. He snatched it up, inserted two shells and handed the gun to David who raced out and shot the animal eighty yards from the front porch. Sam, Robert, and Patrick Oliver along with Isaac, who was painting a sleigh in the basement, all went out to try to drag the animal up the bank. However, it was too heavy, even for all their combined strength. George and Patrick got their skidoos and, with this help, the great animal was pulled up onto the bank.

Two polar bear cubs taking shelter from a storm.

123

All this time snow was blowing, the full moon was out and it was very cold.

Michael Hunter was telling us that he was out on his skidoo the week before when it was snowing so hard that he almost ran right into a polar bear. The bear reared up onto its hind legs, then swerved one way while Michael swerved the other. Then they both ran away from each other in utter terror. Michael said that he eventually stopped and laughed and laughed. He thought that the polar bear probably did the same.

Michael had many stories to tell about life on the trapline when he was a boy. He told about a Native family that got lost in a bitter storm. The parents froze to death, but the children were saved by the dogs sleeping on top of them, keeping them warm until they were rescued. He said that his father kept a diary in the Cree syllabics through all the years that he was on the trapline. Tragically it was lost in the big flood of 1967 and never found.

Michael told us another story about Winisk being the last Eskimo (now Inuit) encampment in Ontario. One time long ago the Indian men of Winisk were away from the settlement, leaving the women and children there. A band of Eskimos came and killed them, taking the settlement over for themselves. When the Cree men returned, they in turn wiped out the invaders and none ever returned to the area. Of course this was Michael's story and I never heard any other tale resembling it.

Like so many of the Winisk children, Michael attended the Albany residential school when he was young. He said that when he was about twelve or fourteen, he went with the priest by paddle canoe, eastward along the Hudson Bay coast to the Sutton River, up the Sutton River to Sutton Lake and then across country to the Ekwan River. The Ekwan led them down to the coast of James Bay, then to the Albany River which took them up to Fort Albany and the school. Michael did not make any comments about the Albany school, but he did send all of his children there for varying lengths of time, until the day school was established at Winisk.

Michael had also paddled westward from Winisk to Fort Severn where he found an old canon ball buried in the mud. He brought us an old brass shell casing which he thought was about a hundred years old. He said that they used these casings over and over again,

Millie standing beside a polar bear skin being stretched out of the reach of the dogs.

lilling and refilling them with shot and powder. He also gave us two iron cutting tools for making the wads that went into the shells. He gave George two shotgun shells made by the Dominion Gun Company, one a twelve gage and one a sixteen gage. George hoped to set these artifacts up in the school as the beginning of a collection, along with samples of beadwork and moccasins.

Mike Hunter was a nephew of Michael's. Some of his children went to school at Albany while some of the older boys followed their father on the trapline. One autumn day his second oldest boy, Charlie, was drowned at Albany after a group of boys had asked permission to go off into the bush. They had not said anything about going skating. When two of the boys broke through the ice, the others tried to shove a canoe out to them, but Charlie Hunter could not hold on and slipped beneath the ice.

At this time, Mike and his family were out on the trapline somewhere on the Sutton River with his oldest boy, George, and two preschoolers. His wife was also expecting another child. Since a

Above. Ivan and Danion are Winisk brothers who soon will learn to hunt, a vital skill in the north.
Left. A polar bear skin dries, out of the reach of the dogs.

helicopter from the oil drilling rig in Hudson Bay was flying around in the area, it was diverted to Mike's camp to bring him and his family back. Michael asked if he could go and be the one to break the bad news to them, but there wasn't room for him in the helicopter, a great disappointment to him. Eventually the Hunter family was located and transported to Moosonee. There the body was buried, after being brought back from Timmins where an autopsy had been performed.

Life in the North had its perils and its rewards. Our time there enriched our understanding of the meaning of life.

OF DOGS AND MEN

We should never have done it. When we left for Christmas two families asked us to bring two dogs back with us. They believed they needed new canine blood in the settlement. The Humane Society in Toronto refused to let us buy two of their dogs because, when they heard of their destination, they were concerned as to how we could get medical help to the animals if it were required. They expressed no interest about how we could get medical help for ourselves, which is probably the way it should be.

Some little pups had been born on a neighbouring farm. Just before we left for Winisk in the fall, George picked out two small ones of indeterminate lineage and arranged to transport them into the north. Air Canada regarded them as just so much baggage. We paid seventeen dollars for a cage in which to convey them and then sixteen dollars for their tickets. During the hour and a half flight to Timmins, the dogs travelling in the baggage section were pretty air sick. At the airport they were unloaded and left outside in twenty degree weather, all wet and unprotected, while the baggage was transported to the terminal. By the time we retrieved the pups they were pretty messy, but George washed them in the terminal washroom and mopped up the floor afterwards. Austin Airways agreed to keep them over night and somebody, we never knew who, looked after them very well, taking them outside for a run before closing up for the night.

Hoping to fly to Moose Factory the next day, we arrived at the airport before dawn, to find that the weather was too bad for flying. We waited till noon only to be told we would have to return the following day. This time we didn't leave the dogs, but took them to the hotel where they were received with tolerance, with permission given for us to keep the dogs in our room in the bath tub. It meant, of course, that we couldn't take a bath which we much needed. Nor could we flush the toilet in the night for fear the sound would wake the dogs and they would start to howl.

Fortunately the next day brought good flying weather. One and a half hours from departure we were in Moose and some three

128

hours later at Winisk. As usual we went from the base to the village by skidoo, with me and the dogs under a tarpaulin, all doing just fine. The one dog was placed in a good home with an elderly lady who let him be a house dog. The other one they called Smokey became an outside dog tied to a stake on the river bank. It broke our hearts.

But in a village where life was tough for everyone, the care of mere dogs was low priority. Our caretaker had a little dog called Three which had pups in the middle of February, in frigid weather with a storm blowing up. George and I took a bucket of food down to her, along with a box for shelter. I tried to crawl to where she was, but could see nothing, not even with a flashlight although I could hear the pups squealing. We were unable to position the box under the house, but left it at the side, along with the food and hoped Three would find them. After a storm such as this one the outside dogs would all be covered with a blanket of white, probably good insulation. At the same time our neighbour did not object to us taking Smokey inside now and then out of the cold.

One Saturday in early spring, while George was over at the base and some ladies were down in the basement doing a washing, I looked out the window and saw the big white dog called Junior lying at Alex's door. He had been a magnificent creature all white and yellow with a waving tail, who used to cavort around with his mother and the other dogs, providing the greatest entertainment. Sometimes he would scratch at the door, but usually was too nervous to come in. Two small dogs would rush in instead. He was so dependent on his mother , Three, and so nervous of people that some called him 'Chicken.' We were all so fond of him, despite his odd behaviours. But Mary Gull had shot him because, she said, he had stolen some food from the cache she had on poles outside her house and for a time he had disappeared from the village. Now he could only drag himself along on his two front legs, his back having been paralysed by the bullet. He had been missing for over a week and was now weak and groggy.

A number of little boys were playing baseball all around him, not paying any attention to the injured dog. I went over and patted his head, then took a dish of food to him and later sent him some milk by way of Joseph. Although a storm was blowing up I did not know what else I could do, but cried all day seeing the dog lying by the door so helpless and ill. I tried to reach George by phone at the base, but he was away out among the buildings and nobody could get him. Maybe they didn't try. Finally I fell into bed in an uneasy sleep and woke up by throwing up with a queasy stomach.

When George came home I fell into his arms and tried to choke out the story, pointing out the helpless animal lying across the trail, by this time trying to crawl back into the bush. George put me down on the couch, put a single shell in his rife and went out. A few minutes later I heard a shot and the beautiful animal's agony was over. Mine still remains.

One time Remi Stoney grabbed up a small pup by two legs and threw it over a high bank into the river. The pup hit the stoney beach, rolled into the water and dragged itself back onto the beach shivering with cold. Some larger dogs hurried down, surrounded the small animal, sniffing at it and trying to lick it dry. Even their furry bodies surrounding the pup helped keep it warm in the icy wind. What compassion the people lacked, the dogs tried to supply.

One time Alex had a dog tied up in the pouring rain. George got a large box which he gave to Luke to provide shelter for the dog. The dog spent most of his time sitting on top. With Smokey tied outside our neighbour's house, George got one of the big wooden reels left by the telephone company men, and cut a hole in it for a door. He set it outside for Smokey to use as a dog house. Like the other dog, Smokey seemed to prefer to sit on top.

One spring afternoon, members of Treaty Nine were in for band business when George was trying to figure out how to save a little dog that Theresa Mack had shot. He found the dog lying at the side of the road, so he picked it up and took it into Daniel Gull's house nearby. The dog, a cute little thing, belonged to Albert who was out in Toronto at the time. George thought that if he put the animal in a splint, it just might recover. When he went out to his skidoo to get some materials, he found Mrs. Mack there with Susan Koostachin. Mrs. Mack said she had not wanted the dog to die, but she didn't want George to attend to it. She then pulled a knife and held it up threateningly. George had little difficulty taking the knife away, but decided it might be better to go home and call Daniel Gull down to the house to explain to him what he thought should be done. When Daniel arrived he said that the dog had died, no doubt killed according to what they thought was the wiser course.

Later Albert acquired another dog from Fort Severn, but it arrived in an unhealthy state, with some kind of outbreak all around its mouth and even at its rectum. He brought it to George who gave it a shot of penicillin which he procured from Father Daneau, along with some healing salve. George then phoned a veterinary in Timmins for advice. He was very helpful. For a while George kept the dog in a box in our basement, then returned it to Albert when it had recovered sufficiently. We never did find out what the problem actually was.

By now Smokey had been in the settlement about two years, growing into a large, sturdy dog. We fed him frequently, took him into the house from time to time whenever our neighbours let him off his chain. The summer we were out they told us that Smokey sat on our porch all summer, his eyes glued to the river, undoubtedly hoping for our return. We did return to claim him but not just yet.

There had been a rumour of rabies in the settlements around the bay and a government man of some sort arrived to give rabies shots to all of the dogs of the village. Unfortunately he was so drunk that he could barely stand up, let alone give shots of any kind. George happily took over the enterprise, passing the word that people were to bring their dogs to the school, and George would administer the required shots. They did. Dog after dog arrived in one kind of restraint or another. I could picture the dogs rolling up their fur in preparation for the shots, but George said that was not the way it happened. The next day the man who should have been giving the shots had recovered sufficiently to get on the plane for home with all his equipment, uncertain as to whether the job had been done or not.

One winter's day George and I went for a skidoo ride through the village, with George driving the machine and me in the sleigh behind. On the point where the road entered the bush a group of very unfriendly dogs descended upon us, leaping and snapping at George. decided I should jump out of the sleigh and give him a hand at driving them away. I tried kicking at the dogs, but one

George drives some of his pupils to school by snowmobile.

sneaked up behind and gave me a good bite on the leg. In alarm George tossed me back into the sleigh and headed for home where he washed and bandaged what turned out to be quite a nasty bite. So was I going to get rabies? George thought I might, although he was less than sympathetic.

"I told you not to get out of the sleigh," was his totally unhelpful comment.

A few days later I was relieved to see a plane arriving in the settlement with medical people on board. I quickly sought out the nurse to tell her that I had been attacked by a vicious dog and was probably at serious risk of rabies. But she had more interesting things on her mind, describing in great detail her recent engagement to the dentist at Moosonee.

"We're getting married next month," she told me, "and then we are leaving for…" (dear knows where).

"But I got bit by one of the dogs," I repeated, rolling up my pant leg to show her.

"And the girls at the hospital had a lovely shower for me and they gave me…" and on and on she went.

Smokey and dogs were indispensible to life in the North.

I finally decided that if I was going to start frothing at the mouth I had better do it right away if I was ever going to get her attention. Of course it didn't happen then nor subsequently. I sighed, pulled down my pant leg and went home, trusting that the nurse married her dentist and lived happily ever after.

OUR LAST BREAKUP

———— ◼ ————

Freezeup and breakup were always times of tension, indicating that the village would be cut off from outside communication for from two to six weeks. Breakup was particularly hazardous. If the ice broke up at the mouth of the Winisk River before it broke upstream, all would be well. If, however, the reverse were the case and the ice broke upstream while the mouth of the river was still solid, the water and ice flowing downstream had no place to go except to spread over the flatlands and inundate anything in its path. The water was not the major hazard, but the chunks of ice, many as large as houses would sweep across the village, smashing everything in its path.

Before breakup in the spring many of the people left the village and went out into the bush to wait until it was over. Those who stayed in the village tied their boats to their doors when they sensed that breakup was near. A boat would be accessible if the village were flooded. The two buildings with basements were our house and the mission, both of which were able to withstand most floods even when all other buildings were swept away. The night of breakup, therefore, these two places were filled people. In our house Alex's younger children came to sleep, along with their elderly grandfather and a few other people with babies and young children. They slept where they could, on the couch, in back bedrooms and so on until morning came and the river was once more flowing freely, albeit awash with blocks of ice. No one could cross the river until the ice was gone.

I always slept soundly through breakup, perhaps because I was not aware of just how deadly it could be. Most of the people in the village were more apprehensive than I was, remembering previous floods when the swift flowing water and the great bergs of ice swept over them, smashing their homes and inundating everything in its path.

During the flood of 1967, most of the houses, along with the Hudson's Bay Company store were carried back into the bush, the store riding so gently that not even a lamp globe was broken,

134

Blocks of ice from the Winisk River.

according to the story told by the manager. However, many of the canned goods lost their labels and customers had to take a chance on what they were buying. Would the contents be peaches, beans, soup or something else?

Three years after we left, the big flood of 1976 struck, wiping out the entire village and drowning two people. Seventy-six year old Johnny Crowe could not reach his canoe in time and was swept away by the icy waters. Margaret Chookamolin, mother of three children, managed to save the two older ones, but was caught in the flood waters with the baby. Holding him above her, she tried to swim to where her sister was trying to reach her in a canoe. The sister was able only to catch the baby as they swept by. The mother disappeared under the waves and was drowned.

Father Daneau wrote to me describing his plight in the flood:

"In my rectory was like in the middle of a river, ice drifting in both sides of the house. A chunk of ice smashed my stairs and the veranda. Another piece of ice made a big hole on one side of the house.

135

As breakup nears, each family ties its boat to the front door in readiness for a flood.

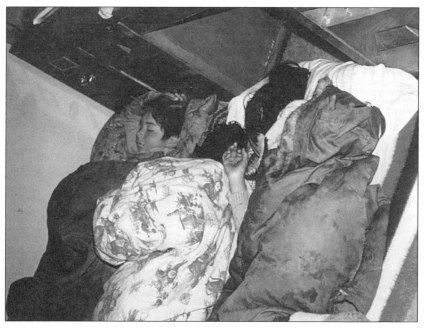

Three boys sleep on the floor at the teacher's house the night of the breakup.

The ice flows down the Winisk River to Hudson Bay for days after the ice breaks up. There is a boat with two men in it in the distance, but it is very dangerous to navigate the ice.

All the windows of the basement were smashed, the basement is still full of ice. When we had a foot of water on the first floor I was obliged to move to the second floor. For a while I was in real danger but I did not realize what was happening. I was too busy trying to save books which I was soon obliged to abandon."

"All communication was cut, we had no electricity, no phone but a man from Telesat was able to send a message by satellite. In less than three hours a helicopter came to our rescue. The helicopter picked up the people scattered in the bush and brought them to the airport…. "

"The helicopter came to take me around eight o'clock. It landed on the ice near the front door. Water was already down from seven to three or four feet, the danger was away. I decided to stay in the house for the night. As a matter of fact I stayed till Sunday morning and then after celebrating a last mass in Winisk I flew to Moosonee, stopping in Attawapiskat to see my people."

The people never went back to Winisk after that, but were evacuated to Attawapiskat where they stayed with friends and

137

relatives until a new village called Peawanuck (the Cree word for flint) was built some thirty miles upstream, where the danger of flood was virtually nonexistent. There a new air strip was built along with new houses, a new school, church and community hall and where the people now live in much greater security.

Apprehensive of the dangers of breakup, the couple who taught the adults at Winisk, came in one night along with the store manager and stayed till late talking about the possibility of breakup that night. Since we didn't encourage them to spend the night with us, they eventually went home although Jim (the adult teacher) apparently sat up all night waiting for disaster to occur. Nothing happened.

The only thing that happened was that Tom, the store manager, phoned us in great excitement at four in the morning to say that the river ice had broken and the water was rising. We got up and looked up and down the river, but all we could see was Jim and Fred on the foggy bank staring down at the river. Nobody else was in sight, and since we could see no water, we went back to bed. George wanted to pour a pail of water in under Jim's door, but I wouldn't let him.

Nearly a week later the ice did begin breaking, with about half the river on our side flowing freely while the other half from the middle to the far bank was still frozen. Great chunks of ice would break off and float downstream like small icebergs giving off a chilly breeze. The night before, Fred had phoned about 11:00 p.m. to say that the bank was crowded with people watching the breakup. Again we looked out and couldn't see anybody, except Fred running up and down all by himself. The only other object on the bank was a garbage can incinerator.

The evening before breakup, George and I had taken a walk onto the flats at the lower end of the river, but all the while keeping watch in case a flood did come suddenly. We then would have to make a run for it to the bank which rose in the distance, lined with poplars and evergreens. The flats were all muddy with clay and wide outcroppings of willows. Stretches of open water lay everywhere, where ducks flounced up and down on the surfaces. George had his gun with him and took shots at them from a crouched position in the willows but hit nothing. My heart was with the ducks and I was glad they escaped. They were small birds whose wings flip-flopped as high above them as below them as they flew. Now and then scout birds seemed to wing above us as though spying out the land and then reporting to the main groups. A few seagulls floated about too, while a thin stream of the river flowed steadily below them. Here and there big chunks of frozen snow lay in the shallows, left by the retreating water making the air chilly.

But this was to be our last breakup. The time had come for us to leave the north and settle on a farm in the south, where medical attention would be available for my eye when it was needed and for George's heart which had long troubled us both.

For the most part we had enjoyed the unfailing kindness of the people of Winisk, in spite of the differences in our backgrounds and the misunderstandings that often resulted. The people seemed to allow for our ineptitude and sometimes the errors that followed. George had taught among the Native people of the north for nearly twenty years and I had lived and worked among them for about the same time. But still we made mistakes, perhaps exacerbated by the stress of isolation and dependency on bureaucracy and other agencies that lay beyond our control. We hoped the people would forget and forgive as they seemed to do so generously.

From time to time they would bring us gifts according to what they had—a beaded purse, a pair of moccasins, a mitten cord, a chunk of caribou, a goose all plucked and cleaned and pinned together with a feather. The size of George's feet had been a continuing source of amusement, especially to the women who made him moosehide moccasins. Little girls would put a doll in one of his moccasins and dangle it down their backs in imitation of a tikinagan. One of the Oblate Fathers regarded George's feet with amazement: "Size fourteen!" he exclaimed, "Two times my size,"and he gazed down at his little size sevens.

On one of his birthdays, I had happened to give Father Daneau a birthday serviette when he came for Sunday night supper. Unknown to us he passed the word that it was George's birthday. As a result that night a group of people all assembled in the house, bringing gifts and singing, "Happy Birthday." The children as they returned to school after lunch entered singing the same song, as did our friend Albert who delivered it over the telephone. There were so many memories.

I couldn't say goodbye to those who were such close friends and with whom I had shared so much for so long. I knew I could not go from house to house, as George would later do, shaking hands and saying farewell, knowing that the children would be growing up, getting married and having children of their own, and I would know nothing of them. Although I was ashamed to do so, I slipped away one day when a chartered plane came in and the pilot said I could leave with him and his passenger.

Alex took me and the other passenger across the river, knowing full well I was trying so hard not to burst into tears. He quietly left me at the far shore where the truck was waiting to take us to the plane at the base and for the last time into the outside world. I watched Alex as long as I could see him, and he held my gaze until he disappeared around the first island and was gone. I turned, boarded the vehicle, and headed to my new life among what might be called my own people. A major part of my life remained behind.

When I arrived home in the south, I first had to attend to some urgent business relating to our purchase of a farm located near George's brother. George phoned me every day even though I told him not to because of the expense. He would agree that he would not phone any more, then the next night he would again be on the telephone.

On one such call he said that our neighbour had suggested that if he would like to take Smokey back south he could do so. By this time Smokey was a large, heavy animal, and not one you could easily transport along with all one's other gear.

"You can't take him all the way off Hudson Bay," I remonstrated, "It would be kinder to put him to sleep than leave him there."

George agreed. He made a ball of goose meat, which he stuffed with digitalis pills which would stop Smokey's heart, and went out onto the river bank to give it to him. When Smokey saw him, he leapt with joy and threw himself into George's arms.

"I couldn't do it," George told me. He tossed the meat into the river, untied Smokey and decided to bring him home. It meant taking Smokey, along with his other baggage, into a canoe to cross the river, up into a truck where he bit one of the men, and then into the plane to Moosonee.

"You can't take that dog with you without a muzzle or a cage," declared the clerk as George boarded. George just held onto Smokey's collar and lifted him on board where he held him firmly under the seat. The clerk was too cowed to object. At Moosonee he took Smokey for a run then loaded him onto the plane for Timmins.

"You can't take that dog on board the plane like that," declared the baggage clerk as he saw George approaching. Without a word George lifted the dog on board with him and again held him under the seat all the way to Timmins.

From Timmins to Toronto, George was taking the train. "You can't take that dog on board," declared the baggage man, "without a muzzle or a cage." George loaded Smokey on board just the same, offering to stay with him in the baggage car all the way to Toronto. That would not be allowed, so they tied Smokey in the baggage car where he chewed apart every rope they used. George went down to be with him as often as they would let him, neither he nor the dog getting any sleep all the way to Toronto.

I met them at the Union Station and two sorrier looking specimens would have been hard to find. George had several day's growth of beard, while Smokey was frantic and bewildered. I decided to stop at Yorkdale shopping plaza while George took Smokey out for a much needed run, since he would never make a mess on the train. George walked him up and down the outside plaza, finally sitting down to rest at the last pillar. Smokey hit every pillar along the way, finally George from collar to waist when he reached the last one. But George was too weary to care.

While our house was being built we stayed with George's brother, Carman, where Smokey was tied up with Carman's female dog who thought Smokey was a gift from heaven. The feeling was not mutual.

When we took him to the vet's for a checkup, the vet asked curiously, "Does this dog eat well?"

"He has been nearly starved for two years," we admitted. "But he will never be hungry again."

When we moved to our own place I swore Smokey would never

be tied up again either, but would be free to run at will over our one-hundred and ninety acres. In an amazingly short time he learned where his boundaries lay and never put a foot over the line whether we were at home or not. Although it was George who had brought him on the long journey home, Smokey decided he was my dog, and I was his responsibility. Always he would sit, very alert, between me and any stranger who happened along. When lively music came over the radio and George grabbed me to have a dance, Smokey would jump up and bite George on the leg. I tried to explain to him that George was not hurting me, but that we were having a good time. Smokey would have none of it. As soon as we got up to dance George got another chomp on the leg.

"That dog's a Methodist," George finally concluded, "He doesn't believe in dancing." I was willing, but George declared he was not going to get bitten on the leg every time he tried.

Though we often thought of the north, George and I settled into our new life with enthusiasm. Often late at night Albert or one of the other people would telephone with a hearty "Hello George!" and tell us what was happening at Winisk. Sometimes they would write and enclose pictures of new spouses and new babies and new homes built at Peawanuk after the big flood at Winisk.

On the farm, George and I roamed the fields as we had once explored the tundra and felt the two were much alike. Smokey of course went with us, delirious with happiness that we were all together as he felt we should be.

Suddenly one day in the barn George's heart just stopped beating. I could not believe he was gone. In spite of all logic, for weeks I kept checking the kitchen clock to determine when I should start his lunch or dinner. I finally had to stop the clock entirely. For a long time I was afraid to leave the farm, even to take the short trip into town in case he should come back and I would not be there to meet him. But I still felt his presence as I walked the old paths and admired the trees and birds that he loved so well. Smokey walked with me all the way, a little puzzled why we were only two.

When the news of George's death reached the north, Father Daneau held a requiem mass where the people grieved his loss. The Mennonite people who had long been his friends held a memorial service, as did the Evangelical group led by the Native man George used to teach when he was a boy, and who was now a clergyman.

Smokey was now my only companion. He kept as close as he could to my side, laying his head on my knee when my pain and loss seemed more than I could bear. Our farm was in a beautiful but isolated area with no neighbours and no other lights from horizon to horizon. Over the fields Smokey followed me, especially when the cows were calving. Late at night when the fields were pitch black, he walked by my side while I tried to find some cow that in trouble and bellowing her distress. I had no fear as long as he was there. When storms were blowing on winter nights and I felt an urgency to check the barn once more, Smokey would struggle through the snow at my heels and wait until was I sure that all was well.

One night a police car came up the lane with his red light flashing, on some errand unrelated to me. After he had explained his mission the policeman sat at his car door trying to make friends with Smokey who would have none of him. I tried to help. "Now you go over and make friends with the nice policeman," I urged while the policeman called in his most engaging voice. Smokey just sat at my side and made disapproving growls and never moving an inch.

"As long as you have a dog like that," the policeman smiled, "you are all right." I knew it was true.

Eventually I had to sell the farm and move to town. I took Smokey with me, but he was not his old self. He was growing old with increasing arthritis making movement difficult. Eventually I called the vet who examined him on the kitchen floor and shook her head.

"I can't make him happy," she concluded and I knew she was right.

I held his great head in my arms as she administered the unavoidable injection, and he was gone. Gone with him was a large part of my life with George and with the north and the Native people, but for ever in my heart and memory they will remain, surrounded by my love and undying gratitude.

Mildred Young Hubbert standing outside a Smoke tent.

MILLIE'S LEGACY

▦

Mildred Young Hubbert, 'Millie' to many, was one of those unfor-
gettable individuals whose style and accomplishments had an
enormous impact on everyone with whom she had contact. From
radio listeners who delighted in her larger than life stories to readers of her several books in print, Millie's sizeable following never
knew quite what to expect. But they could always count on being
entertained.

During the final year of her life, she and I were to enjoy a pub-
lisher/author relationship that centred on the eventual publication
of this particular book. How surprised and delighted Millie was
when she discovered my personal familiarity with her beloved
Winisk, as a result of my own stop-over at Father Gagnon's mission home; the very same priest and former neighbour so frequently mentioned in her writings.

One did not need to know Millie long or especially well to rec-
ognize that her entire life was comprised of extraordinary
episodes, constant adventures were the norm. Little wonder that
stories involving Millie's adventure-filled past set the tone at the
large reception following her burial service. Afterwards, as I
walked to my car, a Markdale neighbour and friend of Millie's
remarked: "You know some of us are going to have to keep up the
tradition of hospitality and party giving Millie was noted for." To
which the neighbour added, "She was the catalyst that brought so
many of us together and we must continue her legacy."

The encouragement to follow through with the publication of
Millie's "Winisk" manuscript came from many sources, notably
executors, family and friends. Their interest and that of the Grey
County Historical Society is much appreciated by the publisher.

The publication of "Winisk: On the Shore of Hudson Bay" is
but part of Mildred Young Hubbert's legacy. Hopefully more of
her unpublished works will be in print in future.

Barry L Penhale,
Publisher

Spider and Space

A spider has a line across
To keep me from my door,—
A silver filament of floss
That was not there before.

I saw him when I turned the knob
Dropping from the roof;
I guessed he had begun a job
And now I had the proof.

No warden e'er hung tasselled silk
More carefully about,
To keep the public and my ilk
From Holy Sanctum out.

My dinner inside waited me,
My hands and feet were cold.
This was the grave contingency
That made my spirit bold.

I over-reached the silken rope
That held a world in place,
An dashed a long-surviving hope
That spiders have in space!

George R. Hubbert
Winisk

Under the Arctic Sun

The dunes reflect the morning light
In undulating blue and white,
As they kiss away the Polar night
And hail the Arctic sun.

A million miles of glistening snow
Scatter ice dust to and fro,
And toss it back in the morning glow
To dance in the Arctic sun.

The tundra touches skylines blue,
Where needled bushlands pierct it through,

And winter clouds the heavens strew,
In league with the Actic sun.

The trees stand stiff and dark and green,
With snow-blue hummocks in between,
And the narrow trail where the wolf has been
Following the Arctic sun.

And all alone on muffled feet,
The hunter treads the silent street,
Where heaven and earth and nature meet
And meld in the Arctic sun.

Mildred J. Young
Winisk
January 1973

Parting

My heart is heavy as the winds
That o'er the Barrens blow;
My heart is heavy as the miles
That, unrelenting, grow;
My heart is heavy as the snow
That on the tundra lies;
My heart is heavy with the pain
Of many sad Good-byes.

Don't let me say, Good-bye, my love!
Don't let me say, Good-bye!
For all too late and all too soon
In parting we shall die!

Toronto
August 1972

MILDRED YOUNG HUBBERT
(1924–1997)

Roman Pylypcak

Though the city of Toronto was the author's birthplace, it was both the near and far northern regions of Canada that figured most prominently in the early life of Mildred Young Hubbert. As a teacher and eventually a specialist concerned with the education of Native children, she lived among Native people in the Yukon, the NorthWest Territories and the James and Hudson Bay regions of Northern Ontario.

The author and editor of several books, Millie Hubbert was also a frequent contributor to CFOS Radio in Owen Sound and to CBC Radio, Toronto. She was a favourite with Open Line program host, Dave Carr and with Tom Allen, the host of CBC Radio's weekend morning program, Fresh Air. With Millie as guest, such radio personalities could always count on entertaining air time.

Retirement in 1974 (not that she ever really retired), found Millie and her husband, George Hubbert, enjoying a farm property near Markdale, Ontario. But it was short-lived due to George's death in 1981, at 63 years of age.

Leaving the farm, Millie Hubbert moved into Markdale and to a new life in small town Ontario. She immediately felt at home and plunged with her customary enthusiasm into many local projects, quickly becoming a driving force in heritage preservation.

Millie instantly came to unabashedly love her adopted home town and could not imagine spending her final years in any other community. Her death from cancer at age 73, robbed Markdale and Grey County of one of its most able promoters.

Endnotes

[1] From letter to Mildred Young Hubbert from Nancy Wilson, Ministry of Natural Resources, Moosonee; February, 1977

[2] The American Edgar Bergen, a well-known ventriloquist with his 'stage wooden dummy' Charlie McCarthy, became famous during the golden age of radio. Today his daughter Candice Bergen is a noted television personality.

[3] Margaret A. Carrell, *Science, History and Hudson Bay, Vol. 2.* (Department of National Defence, 1968) p 926; Polar Bear Provincial Park, Background Information, p. 43.

[4] *Moccasin Telegraph*, (Hudson's Bay Company Archives, Summer, 1973).

Other Books by Mildred Young Hubbert and George Richard Hubbert

Muskeg, Moss and Me: Mildred J. Young, 1973, 48 pages; A book of poetry about Canada's North and the Native people.

Via Severn to the Bay: George R. Hubbert, 1973, 60 pages; A book of poetry about Canada's North and the Native people.

Winter's at the Gates: Mildred J. Young and George R. Hubbert, 1974, 56 pages. Another book of Northern poetry.

The Home Place: Mildred J. Young and George R. Hubbert, 1980, 48 pages. Poems describing rural life in Grey County.

Since the Day I was Born: Mildred Young Hubbert, 1991, 256 pages. Growing up in southern Ontario.

Into Canada's North, "Because it was There": Mildred Young Hubbert, 1993, 118 pages. Mildred's personal account of her life in the Northwest Territories.

Books Edited by Mildred Young Hubbert

Split Rail Country: Mildred Young Hubbert (editor), 1985, 536 pages. A history of Artemesia Township, Grey County.

Markdale, The Crossroads of Grey: Mildred Young Hubbert (editor), 1988, 380 pages. A history of the Village of Markdale.

The Little Schools of Grey: Mildred Young Hubbert (editor), 1983, 310 pages. A history of Holland Township, Grey County.

INDEX